QUINTESSENTIAL
FILIPINO
COOKING

QUINTESSENTIAL FILIPINO COOKING

75 AUTHENTIC AND CLASSIC RECIPES OF THE PHILIPPINES

LIZA AGBANLOG

FOUNDER OF SALU SALO RECIPES

PAGE STREET
PUBLISHING CO.

PAGE STREET
PUBLISHING CO.

Copyright © 2018 Liza Agbanlog

First published in 2018 by

Page Street Publishing Co.

27 Congress Street, Suite 105

Salem, MA 01970

www.pagestreetpublishing.com

Distributed by Macmillan, sales in Canada by The Canadian Manda Group.

22   21   20   19   18   1   2   3   4   5

ISBN-13: 978-1-62414-548-3

ISBN-10: 1-62414-548-5

Library of Congress Control Number: 2018932151

Cover and book design by Page Street Publishing Co.

Photography by Allie Lehman

Printed and bound in China

To my mom

Contents

INTRODUCTION

My relationship with cooking and food started at an early age. I remember being a young girl and going to the wet market with my older sister, list in hand, to fetch ingredients for my mom to make dinner. While at the market, we would stop and have snacks such as *palabok* (noodles in special sauce) or *banana cue* (caramelized fried banana). When we got home, we would help our mom with preparation and watch her cook. Sometimes, when our mom was busy tending to her store, my sisters and I would do the cooking instead.

Growing up, my mom would mostly cook dishes from her hometown of Gapan, Nueva Ecija, while my dad would make us dishes influenced by his Chinese heritage. I would look forward to coming home from school and eating my mom's *sinigang* (sour soup) or my dad's vegetable and tofu dishes. Our diet consisted mostly of vegetables and fish. The combination of both my parents' cooking styles has been the biggest influence in the way that I cook.

When I got married, my cooking style was further influenced by my mother-in-law. She passed down the recipes that my husband enjoyed growing up. Unlike my mother's dishes that used more vegetables, her recipes tended to use more meat. I am thankful for her expertise because it has broadened my culinary knowledge.

When my family immigrated to Canada, I was suddenly overwhelmed with the necessity to cook for my family. In the Philippines, I was able to rely on my extended family for help in cooking, and taking care of my kids, but in Canada, I was on my own. Cooking Filipino food in Canada was especially challenging at first because some of the ingredients were not easy to find. We had to rely on ourselves and the Filipino community to adapt to change based on which ingredients were available. By combining my existing knowledge with what I learned, I was able to successfully re-create some of my favorite dishes.

I started my blog in June 2012 and it has been a challenging, but fulfilling, experience. Since then, the blog has surpassed what I had initially set out to do. It started as a way to archive the many recipes and cooking styles I had accumulated over my lifetime. I wanted it to be easy to access and wanted to share it with both my family and friends, and other people. I thought that a blog would be the perfect way to capture all of these things. As the blog grew, I was surprised with how many people found it and were willing to share their experiences, too. One thing I didn't anticipate was how many different recipes I'd get to try while experimenting for the blog.

As a humble mother and wife, I never thought I would have my own blog or even my own book. But throughout all the experiences I had growing up and starting my blog, I discovered that I was able to make all the dishes I grew up eating. I wanted to make this book so I could share my recipes with people in a new way, and maybe help others make the Filipino dishes they too grew up eating once upon a time.

LUTUING BABOY AT BAKA

PORK AND BEEF DISHES

Pork is arguably the most popular meat in Filipino cuisine. At any big Filipino gathering, a whole roasted pig, called *lechon*, is generally the centerpiece of the buffet table. It is usually served whole, after being roasted over a fire pit. As is typical in Filipino cooking, no part of the pig goes unused. For example, parts of the head and liver are used to make *sisig* (chopped pork with onion and lemon), while the blood is used to make *dinuguan* (pork blood stew). Other parts of the pig, such as the heart, intestines and kidneys, are also used in Filipino dishes.

Although not as popular as chicken and pork, there are still some dishes in Filipino cooking where beef is the focal point of the dish. Examples of these dishes include *mechado* (beef stew in tomato sauce), *bistek* (beef steak) and *kare-kare* (oxtail stew in peanut sauce).

PORK RIBS ADOBO

These mouth-watering and fall-off-the-bone-tender ribs are one of my family's favorite adobo dishes. I recommend using pork back ribs since they take on the adobo flavor well and will give you more flavorful ribs. Although using pork ribs in this adobo recipe puts a different spin on the Filipino classic, it still uses the simplest approach of cooking adobo. All of the ingredients are combined in the pan and simmered until tender—it doesn't get any easier than that!

YIELD: 4 TO 6 SERVINGS

3 lb (1.3 kg) pork back ribs, cut into individual rib segments

¾ cup (180 ml) white vinegar

½ cup (120 ml) soy sauce

6 cloves garlic, crushed

2 bay leaves

½ tsp freshly ground black pepper

1 cup (240 ml) water, plus more as needed

Combine the pork, vinegar, soy sauce, garlic, bay leaves, pepper and water in a heavy pan and bring to a boil over medium-high heat. Reduce the heat to medium, cover and simmer until the pork is tender, about 1 hour. Stir occasionally and add ½ cup (120 ml) of water each time as needed, making sure the ribs are covered in the sauce.

Uncover the pan and reduce the liquid until it starts to glaze, about 15 to 20 minutes.

Remove the bay leaves. Transfer the ribs onto a serving plate. Pour the sauce over the ribs and serve.

ADOBONG PUTI
(WHITE PORK ADOBO)

This dish gets its name from the fact that there is no soy sauce used. In a typical Filipino adobo dish, soy sauce is used to give it a darker color and salty taste. This version uses salt in place of soy sauce, giving it a lighter color and different flavor. Give this one a try if you are looking for a different take on Filipino adobo.

YIELD: 4 SERVINGS

2 lb (900 g) skinless pork belly or shoulder, cut into 2-inch (5-cm) cubes

2 cups (475 ml) water

½ cup (120 ml) white vinegar

4 cloves garlic, crushed

1 tsp whole peppercorns

2 bay leaves

1 tsp salt

Steamed rice, for serving

In a heavy pan, combine the pork, water, vinegar, garlic, peppercorns, bay leaves and salt. Bring the mixture to a boil over medium-high heat. Reduce the heat to medium, and cook covered until the meat is fork tender, about 1 hour. Check and stir periodically making sure that there is still a good amount of liquid, adding water in ½ cup (120 ml) increments as needed.

When the pork is tender, remove the lid and continue to simmer until most of the liquid has evaporated and the pork starts to render fat, about 12 minutes. Drain the excess oil.

Remove the bay leaves. Serve with steamed rice.

SKINLESS LONGGANISA
(PORK SAUSAGE)

Longganisa is a pork sausage that is typically served for breakfast. Although longganisa can be bought at a Filipino market, making your own longganisa lets you choose what to put in it and gives you room to experiment. This version is skinless and doesn't use any casing; instead, the filling is individually wrapped in wax paper and frozen so that the sausage stays together when cooking. The sausages may be thawed first before frying, or fried frozen instead if you are pressed for time. Either way, these pork sausages are best served with a sunny side up egg for a satisfying breakfast.

YIELD: 28 SAUSAGES

2 lb (900 g) lean ground pork

¼ cup (45 g) brown sugar

1 tsp Worcestershire sauce

3 tbsp (45 ml) soy sauce

1 tsp garlic powder

1 tsp salt

¼ tsp freshly ground black pepper

28 (6 x 6-inch [15 x 15-cm]) sheets of wax paper

Vegetable oil, for frying

Cooked rice, for serving

Fried eggs, for serving

Vinegar Garlic Sauce (page 165), for serving

In a large bowl, combine the ground pork, brown sugar, Worcestershire sauce, soy sauce, garlic powder, salt and pepper. Mix thoroughly.

Place 1½ tablespoons (20 g) of the mixture on a piece of wax paper. Shape the mixture into a log, roll as tightly as you can and twist both ends of the wax paper to seal. Repeat the process for the rest of the mixture.

Place the rolled sausages in a container with a lid and store in the freezer for 2 hours or until ready to cook.

To cook, unwrap the frozen sausages and fry in batches in hot vegetable oil until cooked through, about 5 to 6 minutes per batch. Drain on paper towels.

Serve with rice, a fried egg and Vinegar Garlic Sauce on the side.

NOTE: The frozen sausages may be thawed 2 hours before frying. If you are planning to have it for breakfast, thaw in the refrigerator the night before.

TOKWA'T BABOY
(FRIED TOFU AND PORK)

Tokwa't baboy is an appetizer that you will most likely find at the center of the table, and is usually enjoyed with an ice-cold beer. It can also be enjoyed as a side dish for *lugaw* (congee, or rice porridge). Classically, it is a dish made of cubed fried tofu, boiled chopped pork ears and pork belly, served with a dipping sauce of soy sauce and vinegar on the side. This recipe is a slight variation that uses the same cooking method, but without the pork ears. The soy sauce–vinegar mixture is also incorporated into the dish during cooking.

YIELD: 4 SERVINGS

1 lb (450 g) skinless pork belly, cut in half lengthwise

6 cups (1.4 L) water

2 tsp (11 g) salt

1 onion, peeled and halved

2 bay leaves

1 tsp whole peppercorns

1 cup (240 ml) vegetable oil

1 lb (450 g) firm tofu, drained and patted dry with paper towels

4 tbsp (40 g) minced shallots

2 cloves garlic, minced

1½ cups (350 ml) white vinegar

¼ cup (60 ml) soy sauce

2 tbsp (25 g) sugar

1 Thai chile, minced

Chopped green onions, for garnish

In a large pot, bring the pork belly, water, salt, onion, bay leaves and peppercorns to a boil. Reduce the heat to medium and cook until tender, about 1 hour. Drain the pork and reserve 1 cup (240 ml) of the broth. Let the pork cool slightly and then slice it into bite-size pieces. Set aside.

In a large skillet, heat the oil over medium-high heat. Add the tofu and fry until brown and crispy, about 3 minutes. Drain on paper towels and cut into ½-inch (13-mm) cubes. Set aside.

Remove all but 2 tablespoons (30 ml) of the oil from the pan and place it back over medium heat. Add the shallots and sauté for about 1 minute. Add the garlic and sauté for another 30 seconds. Add the vinegar, soy sauce, sugar, reserved pork broth and Thai chile.

Bring to a boil and stir in the pork belly and tofu. Simmer for a few minutes to allow the pork and tofu to absorb the sauce.

Transfer to a bowl and garnish with green onions.

GROUND PORK MENUDO

Menudo is a Spanish-influenced stew that is popular in Fillipino cuisine. Traditional menudo is commonly eaten for lunch or dinner and consists of cubes of pork simmered in tomato sauce, with vegetables added afterwards. This recipe uses ground pork instead, which is a practical variation and an easy way of making menudo.

YIELD: 4 SERVINGS

2 tbsp (30 ml) olive oil

2 cloves garlic, chopped

1 small onion, chopped

1 lb (450 g) lean ground pork

1 tbsp (15 ml) fish sauce

½ cup (120 ml) tomato sauce

1½ cups (350 ml) water

1 cup (128 g) diced carrots

1 large potato, peeled and diced

1 red or green bell pepper, seeded and diced

½ cup (75 g) frozen green peas

½ cup (75 g) raisins

Salt and freshly ground black pepper, to taste

Steamed rice, for serving

Heat the oil in a skillet over medium-high heat. Add the garlic and onion, and sauté until the onion begins to soften, about 2 minutes.

Add the ground pork and cook, stirring regularly, for 5 minutes or until the meat is lightly browned. Stir in the fish sauce.

Add the tomato sauce and water. Stir, cover and cook on medium heat for 5 minutes, stirring occasionally.

Add the carrots, potato and bell pepper, and cook for 10 minutes. Add the green peas and raisins, and cook for another 5 minutes, or until the vegetables are tender. Season to taste with salt and pepper. Serve with steamed rice.

CRISPY PORK BINAGOONGAN
(CRISPY PORK ᵂᴵᵀᴴ SHRIMP PASTE)

This dish is always a hit when I make it for my family. We like to pair it with eggplant omelets, or with boiled or grilled vegetables. There are many ways to make this dish, but this way of making *binagoongan* is my family's favorite. I learned this method from a family member who I've always thought of as a good cook during my recent visit to the Philippines.

YIELD: 4 SERVINGS

1 lb (450 g) skinless pork belly, cut into 1-inch (2.5-cm) pieces

2 cloves garlic, crushed

1 cup (240 ml) white vinegar

½ cup (120 ml) water

1 tsp whole peppercorns

1 bay leaf

1 cup (240 ml) vegetable oil

2 cloves garlic, chopped

1 small onion, chopped

1 medium tomato, chopped

½ cup (110 g) bagoong (shrimp paste)

Steamed rice, for serving

Grilled vegetables, for serving

In a medium pot, bring the pork, garlic, vinegar, water, peppercorns and bay leaf to a boil. Reduce the heat to medium and cook, covered, until the meat is fork tender, about 30 minutes. Remove the pork from the broth, reserving ¾ cup (180 ml) of the broth. Pat the pork thoroughly dry with paper towels. Set aside.

In a pan, heat the oil over medium-high heat. Add the pork and fry over medium heat until brown and crispy, about 10 minutes. Transfer the pork onto a paper towel–lined plate.

Remove all but 2 tablespoons (30 ml) of oil from the pan. Reheat the oil over medium-high heat. Add the garlic and onion, and sauté until the onion begins to soften, about 2 minutes. Add the tomato and sauté until soft, about 1 minute.

Stir in the crispy pork. Add the shrimp paste and stir to combine. Add the reserved broth and cook, stirring for 1 minute.

Serve with steamed rice and grilled vegetables.

BAKED LECHON KAWALI
(CRISPY PORK BELLY)

Lechon kawali is a popular Filipino dish consisting of pork belly that is boiled until tender and then deep-fried until brown and crispy. This recipe is a variation that uses the oven instead of a deep fryer, but doesn't sacrifice flavor or texture. Using the oven makes this dish easier to prepare and it will still be crispy on the outside, yet moist on the inside.

YIELD: 4 SERVINGS

2 lb (900 g) boneless pork belly, skin on

12 cups (2.9 L) water

6 cloves garlic, crushed

1 tbsp (20 g) salt

2 bay leaves

½ tbsp (5 g) whole peppercorns

Vinegar Garlic Sauce (page 165), for serving

Place the pork and water in a stockpot. Add the garlic, salt, bay leaves and peppercorns, and bring to a boil over medium-high heat. Reduce the heat to medium, and cook until the meat is fork tender, about 1½ hours. Drain the pork belly and discard the broth.

Preheat the oven to 375°F (190°C).

Transfer the pork skin-side up onto a rack placed on a foil-lined baking sheet. Using a fork, poke the pork's skin several times along the surface. Pat the pork thoroughly dry with paper towels.

Bake the pork until brown and crispy, about 2 hours. Let it cool slightly and then slice into serving pieces. Serve with the Vinegar Garlic Sauce.

PORK AFRITADA
(PORK BRAISED IN TOMATO SAUCE)

Afritada is a tomato-based stew made with either chicken or pork and a variety of vegetables. It is similar to *kaldereta*, *mechado* and *menudo* in that they are all tomato-based stews, but this pork afritada is my family's favorite. We can't get enough of the tender pieces of pork and vegetables, especially when we have it with a bowl of rice or bread.

YIELD: 6 SERVINGS

2 lb (900 g) pork shoulder, cut into 2-inch (5-cm) cubes

Salt and freshly ground black pepper

2 tbsp (30 ml) olive oil

2 cloves garlic, chopped

1 small onion, chopped

1 medium tomato, chopped

2 tbsp (30 ml) fish sauce

½ cup (120 ml) tomato sauce

1½ cups (350 ml) water

1 large potato, peeled and cut into 1-inch (2.5-cm) cubes

1 small carrot, peeled and cubed

1 red bell pepper, seeded and cubed

Season the pork with salt and pepper.

Heat the oil in a heavy pan over medium-high heat. Add the garlic and onion, and sauté until the onion begins to soften, about 2 minutes. Add the tomato and sauté until soft, about 2 minutes.

Stir in the fish sauce. Add the pork and sauté until browned and no longer pink, about 5 minutes.

Add the tomato sauce and water, and bring to a boil. Reduce the heat to medium, cover and simmer, stirring regularly and adding more water as needed. Continue to simmer for 45 minutes or until the pork is tender.

Add the potato, carrot and bell pepper, and cook until tender, about 10 minutes. Season to taste with salt and pepper.

KARE-KARE
(OXTAIL WITH VEGETABLES IN PEANUT SAUCE)

Kare-kare is a popular stew known for its distinct and savory peanut sauce. Beyond the sauce, oxtail or pork hock is the main focus and is accompanied by a mixture of fresh vegetables. The more daring and adventurous may also add tripe. Kare-kare is not an everyday dish, but is served during special occasions, events or holidays.

YIELD: 4 TO 6 SERVINGS

3 lb (1.3 kg) oxtail, cut into 2-inch (5-cm) pieces

10 cups (2.4 L) water

1 tsp salt

½ lb (230 g) green beans, trimmed

1 medium Chinese eggplant, cut diagonally into ½-inch (13-mm) pieces

½ lb (230 g) bok choy, cut in half lengthwise and rinsed well

2 tbsp (30 ml) vegetable oil

2 cloves garlic, chopped

1 small onion, chopped

1 tbsp (8 g) annatto powder

1 tbsp (15 g) shrimp paste, plus more for serving

4 tbsp (64 g) smooth peanut butter

2 tbsp (15 g) mochiko (sweet rice flour) dissolved in 2 tbsp (30 ml) water

Steamed rice, for serving

In a stockpot, bring the oxtail, water and salt to a boil. Lower the heat to medium and cook, covered until tender, about 1½ hours. Remove the oxtail from the broth and set aside.

Add the green beans and eggplant to the broth in the pan. Cook for 5 minutes. Add the bok choy and cook until the vegetables are tender, about 2 minutes. Remove the vegetables from the broth and set aside. Reserve 3 cups (700 ml) of the broth.

Heat the oil in a wok or pan over medium heat. Add the garlic and onion, and sauté until the onion begins to soften, about 2 minutes. Add the annatto powder and shrimp paste, and stir to combine. Add the reserved 3 cups (700 ml) of broth, increase the heat to medium-high and bring the mixture to a boil. Add the oxtail and cook for 5 minutes.

Add the peanut butter and cook for 2 minutes. Add the mochiko mixture, and cook until the sauce thickens, about 1 minute. Add the vegetables and cook until heated through, about 2 minutes. Serve hot with steamed rice and sautéed shrimp paste.

NOTE: *Mochiko* is sweet rice powder that is sold at any Asian supermarket. Cornstarch may be used instead.

BEEF MECHADO
(BEEF STEW IN TOMATO SAUCE)

This Spanish-influenced dish consists of slowly simmered beef in a tangy tomato sauce. Chunks of potatoes and bell peppers complete this hearty stew. When making beef *mechado*, it is important that the meat is slowly cooked over a long period of time, which makes it tender and flavorful. Alternatively, mechado can be made with pork or chicken, but beef mechado is the most common.

2 lb (900 g) stewing beef, cut into 1-inch (2.5-cm) cubes

Salt and freshly ground black pepper

4 tbsp (60 ml) vegetable oil, divided

4 cloves garlic, minced

1 onion, chopped

1 cup (160 g) finely chopped tomatoes

3 tbsp (45 ml) soy sauce

2 tbsp (30 ml) lemon or calamansi juice

2 bay leaves

2 cups (475 ml) water, plus more as needed

1 green bell pepper, cut into large chunks

1 red bell pepper, cut into large chunks

2 potatoes, peeled and cut into large chunks

Steamed rice, for serving

Season the beef with salt and pepper.

In a pan, heat 3 tablespoons (45 ml) of oil over medium-high heat. Add the beef and cook in batches until all sides are browned, about 4 minutes per batch. Remove the beef and its juices from the pan and set aside.

Using the same pan, add the remaining 1 tablespoon (15 ml) of oil. Add the garlic, onion and tomatoes. Sauté until the onion begins to soften, about 2 minutes.

Return the browned beef and its accumulated juices to the pan. Add the soy sauce, lemon juice, bay leaves and water. Bring the mixture to a boil, cover and continue to simmer over medium heat until the beef is tender, about 1 hour. Stir periodically and check if there is still a good amount of liquid, adding water in ½ cup (120 ml) increments as needed.

Add the bell peppers and potatoes. Stir and cook covered until the potatoes are tender, about 10 to 12 minutes. Season with salt and pepper to taste.

Remove the bay leaves and serve with steamed rice.

BEEF PARES
(BRAISED BEEF BRISKET)

This popular street food gets its name from the fact that beef is paired with a flavorful broth (*pares* means pair). The seasoned and tender braised beef is first cooked slowly in the broth, then removed. The flavored broth is then served alongside the braised beef. To make it a complete meal, some will serve beef pares with a bowl of garlic rice.

YIELD: 4 SERVINGS

2 lb (900 g) beef brisket or shank, cut into 1-inch (2.5-cm) cubes

12 cups (2.9 L) water

2 medium onions, peeled and halved

1 tbsp (20 g) kosher salt

1 tsp whole peppercorns

2 tbsp (30 ml) olive oil

2 cloves garlic, minced

1 (1-inch [2.5-cm]) piece fresh ginger, peeled and julienned

⅓ cup (80 ml) soy sauce

⅓ cup (60 g) brown sugar

2 pieces star anise

Salt and freshly ground black pepper, to taste

1 tsp cornstarch, dissolved in 1 tbsp (30 ml) water

Chopped green onions, for garnish

Garlic Rice (page 81), for serving

In a stockpot, bring the beef and water to a boil over high heat.

Add the onions, salt and peppercorns. Reduce the heat to medium and simmer covered for 1½ hours, or until the meat is tender. Drain the beef, reserving the broth.

In a skillet, heat the oil over medium-high heat. Add the garlic and ginger, and sauté until the garlic is lightly browned, about a minute. Add the drained beef, soy sauce and sugar and cook, stirring until the sugar has dissolved and the beef is fully coated with the sugar mixture, about 2 minutes. Add 1 cup (240 ml) of the reserved broth and star anise. Bring to a boil, reduce the heat to medium and cook covered for another 5 minutes. Season with salt and pepper to taste. Add the cornstarch mixture to the broth, stirring until the mixture thickens.

Garnish with green onions. Serve with Garlic Rice and a bowl of the hot reserved broth.

PAKSIW NA PATA
(BRAISED PORK HOCK IN VINEGAR AND SOY SAUCE)

Paksiw is a Filipino method of cooking which means "to cook in vinegar." There are many paksiw dishes in Filipino cuisine, and it is quite common to turn leftover dishes into paksiw dishes. For example, leftover *lechon* (whole roasted pig) is turned into *paksiw na lechon*. Here in Canada, I like to turn leftover roast turkey from Christmas or Thanksgiving into paksiw. This recipe uses pork hock—after simmering it in its sweet tangy sauce for a long period of time, it comes out fall-off-the-bone tender!

YIELD: 3 SERVINGS

2 lb (900 g) pork hock, cut into 3 pieces

4 cups (950 ml) water

½ cup (120 ml) white vinegar

¼ cup (60 ml) soy sauce

¼ cup (45 g) brown sugar

2 cloves garlic, crushed

1 tsp whole peppercorns

2 bay leaves

1 tsp salt, plus more to taste

1 oz (28 g) dried banana blossoms or dried lily buds, soaked in water for at least 30 minutes

In a Dutch oven or heavy pan, combine the pork hock, water, vinegar, soy sauce, sugar, garlic, peppercorns, bay leaves and salt. Bring the mixture to a boil. Cook, covered, over medium heat until the pork is tender, about 1½ hours.

Add the banana blossoms and cook until tender, about 5 minutes. Remove the bay leaves. Season to taste with salt, as needed.

LUTUING MANOK

CHICKEN DISHES

As with many cultures around the world, chicken is a popular meat. The way that chicken is used in Filipino cooking reflects the many influences on Filipino culture across its history, including influences from Chinese, Indian, American and Spanish cuisines. For example, the popular dish chicken *afritada* shows Spanish flair, while chicken *mami* has Chinese roots.

In Filipino cooking, no part of the chicken goes unused. Even the intestines and feet are considered delicacies. Filipino chicken dishes are commonly cooked with the bone in for additional flavor. And the meat is often marinated first for even more flavor. It is common with Filipino cuisine to purchase a whole chicken from the market and use the entire thing in the same dish. Whether it is in a tasty soup or a hearty stew, chicken is a staple meat in Filipino cooking.

FRIED CHICKEN

This fried chicken is unique because it is marinated in a Filipino-style adobo sauce. It is then fried and finished off in the oven. The special marinade and cooking technique make this fried chicken very tasty.

3 lb (1.3 kg) mixture of bone-in, skin-on chicken thighs and drumsticks

½ cup (120 ml) white vinegar

½ cup (120 ml) soy sauce

4 cloves garlic, crushed

1 tsp whole peppercorns

2 bay leaves

1½ tsp (8.5 g) salt, divided

1 cup (120 g) all-purpose flour

2 cups (475 ml) vegetable oil

Steamed rice, for serving

In a large resealable bag, combine the chicken, vinegar, soy sauce, garlic, peppercorns, bay leaves and ½ teaspoon of salt. Seal the bag and toss to evenly coat the chicken. Marinate in the refrigerator for 2 hours.

Preheat the oven to 350°F (190°C).

Combine the flour and 1 teaspoon of salt in a shallow dish. Remove the chicken from the marinade and coat thoroughly with the flour mixture.

Heat the oil in a pan over medium heat and working in batches, fry the chicken for about 2 to 3 minutes on each side or until light brown.

Transfer the chicken onto a metal rack set on a foil-lined baking sheet. Bake the chicken for 35 to 40 minutes or until it is cooked through.

Serve hot with steamed rice.

CHICKEN HAMONADO
(CHICKEN IN PINEAPPLE SAUCE)

Pineapple fans should definitely try this chicken *hamonado* dish. Pineapple is the main ingredient in the marinade and makes the chicken sweet, tender and tasty. Pork can also be used to make hamonado, but this chicken version is my favorite!

YIELD: 4 TO 6 SERVINGS

3 lb (1.3 kg) chicken pieces of your choice (thighs, drumsticks or wings)

2 tbsp (30 ml) fish sauce

1 tbsp (15 ml) lemon juice

1 tsp freshly ground black pepper, plus more to taste

2 tbsp (30 ml) vegetable oil

4 cloves garlic, chopped

1 small onion, chopped

1 cup (240 ml) unsweetened pineapple juice

2 tbsp (25 g) sugar

2 tbsp (30 ml) soy sauce

1 (14-oz [398-ml]) can pineapple chunks with juice

Salt, to taste

Steamed rice, for serving

In a large bowl, combine the chicken pieces with the fish sauce, lemon juice and pepper; toss to combine. Cover with plastic wrap and refrigerate for at least an hour. Drain the chicken and discard the marinade.

Heat the oil in a Dutch oven or heavy-bottomed pan over medium-high heat. Add the garlic and onion, and sauté until the onion begins to soften, about 2 minutes.

Add the chicken and sauté until no longer pink, about 5 minutes.

Add the pineapple juice, sugar and soy sauce. Bring to a boil, reduce the heat to medium and simmer covered until the chicken is almost tender, about 20 minutes.

Add the pineapple chunks with juice and continue to simmer until the sauce has reduced and the chicken is tender, about 20 minutes. Season to taste with salt.

Serve with steamed rice.

CHICKEN SALPICAO
(STIR-FRIED GARLIC CHICKEN)

Chicken *salpicao* is the perfect dish to serve on a busy weeknight because it is quick and easy to make. The marinated chicken pieces are stir-fried with mushrooms and garlic to create this classic Filipino dish. Toasted garlic slivers may be used as a garnish.

YIELD: 4 SERVINGS

MARINADE

1½ tbsp (22 ml) oyster sauce

3½ tbsp (52 ml) soy sauce

3 cloves garlic, minced

GARLIC CHICKEN

2 lb (900 g) boneless, skinless chicken thighs, cut into bite-size pieces

2 tbsp (30 ml) vegetable oil

8 oz (230 g) button mushrooms, halved

Toasted garlic, for garnish (see note)

To make the marinade, combine the oyster sauce, soy sauce and garlic in a large bowl. Mix in the chicken. Refrigerate for 1 hour.

In a large skillet, heat the oil over medium-high heat. Add the chicken with the marinade. Cook until the chicken is no longer pink and juices run clear, about 8 to 10 minutes.

Add the mushrooms and sauté until the mushrooms are cooked, about 2 minutes. Garnish with toasted garlic.

NOTE: To make the toasted garlic, peel and thinly slice a whole head of garlic. Fry over medium heat with enough oil to cover the garlic. Cook, stirring occasionally for about 15 minutes until brown, but not burnt. Drain the excess oil.

PATIS WINGS
(CHICKEN WINGS WITH FISH SAUCE)

Patis (fish sauce) is a common ingredient in Filipino cooking. It can typically be found as part of a *sawsawan* (dipping sauce) or added to soups, but this recipe makes use of patis as a marinade. The fried chicken wings are marinated in the salty, sweet and sour sauce to create this irresistible dish.

YIELD: 6 SERVINGS

MARINADE

¼ cup (60 ml) fish sauce

1 tbsp (15 ml) fresh lime juice

2 tbsp (23 g) brown sugar

1 clove garlic, minced

½ tsp red pepper flakes

WINGS

2 lb (900 g) chicken wings, a mixture of wingettes and drumettes

¼ cup (30 g) cornstarch

½ tsp salt

½ tsp freshly ground black pepper

½ tsp paprika

Vegetable oil, for frying

Cilantro, for garnish

To make the marinade, mix together the fish sauce, lime juice, sugar, garlic and red pepper flakes in a large bowl. Add the wings. Marinate for 1 hour in the refrigerator.

Remove the wings from the marinade and pat dry with paper towels. Discard the marinade.

In a medium bowl, mix together the cornstarch, salt, pepper and paprika.

Dip the wings into the cornstarch mixture. Shake off any excess cornstarch.

Heat the oil in a wok or a large frying pan. Add the wings, in batches, and cook for 8 to 10 minutes, turning a few times. Drain the wings on paper towel–lined plates. Garnish with cilantro, if desired.

CHICKEN POCHERO
(CHICKEN *AND* VEGETABLE STEW)

Chicken *pochero* is a hearty stew consisting of chicken and vegetables. The sweetness of the *saba* bananas combined with the acidity of the tomatoes is just perfect. The addition of chickpeas and sausage makes it filling enough to be a meal on its own.

YIELD: 6 SERVINGS

2 lb (900 g) mixture of bone-in chicken thighs and drumsticks

Salt and freshly ground black pepper

2 tbsp (30 ml) olive oil

1 small onion, chopped

2 cloves garlic, chopped

1 tbsp (15 ml) fish sauce

1 cup (240 ml) tomato sauce

3 cups (700 ml) water

1 large potato, peeled and cut into cubes

4 ripe saba bananas (burro bananas) or Thai bananas, peeled and halved

1 (14-oz [398-ml]) can chickpeas, rinsed and drained

1 chorizo sausage, sliced

4 pieces bok choy, halved and rinsed thoroughly

Steamed rice, for serving

Season the chicken with salt and pepper. Set aside.

In a heavy pan, heat the oil over medium-high heat. Add the onion and garlic, and sauté until the onion begins to soften, about 2 minutes.

Add the chicken and sauté until browned and no longer pink, about 4 minutes.

Add the fish sauce and tomato sauce, stir and then add the water. Bring the mixture to a boil, lower the heat and simmer covered for 20 minutes.

Add the potato and simmer for 10 minutes. Add the saba, chickpeas, chorizo and bok choy, and continue to simmer until the potato is tender, about 5 minutes. Season to taste with salt and pepper.

Serve hot with steamed rice.

ADOBONG DILAW
(ADOBO WITH TURMERIC)

Adobong dilaw is one of the many variations of adobo in the Philippines. This particular version is a yellow adobo and originated in the province of Batangas. Adobong dilaw uses the ingredients found in a typical Filipino adobo dish but adds turmeric in place of soy sauce. The use of turmeric gives the dish a distinct yellow color and a different flavor.

YIELD: 4 SERVINGS

2 lb (900 g) bone-in chicken pieces (thighs, drumsticks or wings)

Salt and freshly ground black pepper

2 tbsp (30 ml) vegetable oil

4 cloves garlic, chopped

1 onion, chopped

1 (1-inch [2.5-cm]) piece fresh turmeric, peeled and julienned or 2 tsp (6 g) turmeric powder

1 tbsp (15 ml) fish sauce

½ cup (120 ml) white vinegar

1 cup (240 ml) water

1 tsp whole peppercorns

2 bay leaves

Steamed rice, for serving

Season the chicken with salt and pepper.

In a Dutch oven or heavy base pan, heat the oil over medium-high heat. Add the garlic and onion, and cook until the onion begins to soften, about 2 minutes. Add the turmeric and stir.

Add the chicken and cook, stirring until browned, about 4 minutes. Stir in the fish sauce.

Add the vinegar, water, peppercorns and bay leaves, and bring to a boil. Reduce the heat to medium and simmer covered for 20 minutes, stirring occasionally.

Remove the lid and continue cooking for 10 minutes, or until the sauce has reduced and thickened. Season with salt and pepper, to taste.

Remove the bay leaves and serve with steamed rice.

CHICKEN BICOL EXPRESS
(SPICY CHICKEN IN COCONUT MILK)

Bicol express is a spicy stew named after a train in the Bicol region of the Philippines. The Bicol region is known for its spicy food and this dish is a perfect example. Although Bicol express is traditionally made with pork, the use of chicken in this dish makes it healthier without sacrificing any flavor.

YIELD: 5 SERVINGS

2 tbsp (30 ml) vegetable oil, divided

3 cloves garlic, minced

1 onion, diced

1 tomato, diced

2 lb (900 g) chicken breast, cut into 1-inch (2.5-cm) cubes

1¾ cups (410 ml) coconut milk

3 finger-length green or red Thai chiles or a mixture of both, minced

1 tbsp (15 g) sautéed shrimp paste

Steamed rice, for serving

In a large skillet, heat 1 tablespoon (15 ml) of the oil over medium-high heat. Add the garlic and sauté for about 1 minute.

Add the onion and tomato. Continue to sauté until the onion is translucent, about 5 minutes.

Add the remaining 1 tablespoon (15 ml) of oil. Add the chicken and sauté until the chicken is no longer pink, about 10 minutes.

Add the coconut milk and bring to a boil. Lower the heat to medium and simmer for 12 minutes or until the chicken is cooked through, stirring periodically.

Stir in the Thai chiles and simmer for 2 minutes. Remove from the heat and stir in the shrimp paste. Serve over steamed rice.

CHICKEN KALDERETA
(CHICKEN IN TOMATO LIVER SAUCE)

Kaldereta is a popular Filipino dish served during parties and holidays. It traditionally uses goat meat as the main ingredient, but beef, chicken and pork may also be used. It is similar to *afritada* and *mechado* which are both Spanish-influenced dishes. These dishes are all tomato-based, and potatoes and bell peppers are the common vegetables. Liver sauce, however, is the distinguishing ingredient in kaldereta.

YIELD: 4 TO 5 SERVINGS

MARINADE

2 tbsp (30 ml) lemon juice

2 tbsp (30 ml) soy sauce

¼ tsp freshly ground black pepper

4 cloves garlic, crushed

CHICKEN

2 lb (900 g) mixture of bone-in chicken thighs and drumsticks

2 tbsp (30 ml) olive oil

1 small onion, chopped

2 cloves garlic, chopped

1 tbsp (15 ml) fish sauce

1 cup (240 ml) tomato sauce

2 bay leaves

2 cups (475 ml) water

1 red bell pepper, diced

1 large potato, peeled and diced

1 small carrot, peeled and diced

¼ cup (52 g) canned liver spread

½ cup (67 g) pitted green olives

Salt and freshly ground black pepper, to taste

Grated cheddar cheese, optional

To make the marinade, combine the lemon juice, soy sauce, pepper and garlic in a bowl. Add the chicken and mix well. Cover and marinate in the refrigerator for 1 hour. Drain the chicken and discard the marinade. Set aside.

In a heavy pan, heat the oil over medium-high heat. Add the onion and garlic, and sauté until the onion begins to soften, about 2 minutes. Add the chicken and sauté until lightly browned, about 4 minutes. Add the fish sauce, stir and then add the tomato sauce, bay leaves and water. Bring to a boil, lower the heat and simmer covered for 25 minutes.

Add the red pepper, potato and carrot. Cover and continue to cook for 10 minutes. Add the liver spread and green olives. Stir and cook until the vegetables are tender, about 5 minutes. Season to taste with salt and pepper.

Remove the bay leaves. Transfer to a serving plate and top with grated cheese, if using.

CHICKEN BARBECUE

A Filipino barbecue is not complete without chicken barbecue. Filipino-style barbecue marinade is known for its sweet and tangy flavor, and this marinade is just that. Marinating the chicken overnight is preferred to get the tastiest results possible. Chicken thighs are used as they are not easily overcooked and result in tastier barbeque.

YIELD: 18 SKEWERS OR 6 SERVINGS

3 lb (1.3 kg) boneless, skinless chicken thighs

5 cloves garlic, minced

¼ cup (60 ml) lemon or calamansi juice

½ cup (120 ml) soy sauce

⅓ cup (80 ml) sweet chili sauce

½ cup (120 ml) ketchup

1 cup (240 ml) lemon lime soda

BASTING SAUCE

½ cup (120 ml) soy sauce

¼ cup (45 g) brown sugar

¼ cup (60 ml) sweet chili sauce

½ cup (120 ml) ketchup

18 (10-inch [25-cm]) bamboo skewers, soaked in water for at least 1 hour before using

Cooked rice, for serving

Achara (page 170), for serving

Prepare the chicken by slicing each thigh crosswise into 1-inch (2.5-cm) thick strips.

In a large resealable bag, combine the garlic, lemon juice, soy sauce, chili sauce, ketchup and lemon lime soda.

Add the chicken, seal and toss to coat the chicken completely. Marinate in the refrigerator overnight.

To make the basting sauce, combine the soy sauce, brown sugar, sweet chili sauce and ketchup in a bowl. Mix well and then set aside.

Thread the chicken pieces onto skewers, around 3 pieces on each stick.

Prepare an outdoor gas or charcoal barbecue over medium heat. Grill the chicken, turning and basting every couple of minutes, until cooked through, about 12 to 15 minutes.

Serve with rice and Achara on the side.

CHICKEN INASAL
(GRILLED LEMONGRASS CHICKEN)

Chicken *inasal* is a grilled chicken dish originating from Bacolod, a city in the Philippines. The marinated chicken is grilled and brushed with annatto oil to give it a distinct color and taste. Serve this tasty grilled dish with Vinegar Garlic Sauce (page 165) and Achara (page 170) and you will have a sure hit!

YIELD: 4 SERVINGS

4 chicken leg quarters

Salt and freshly ground black pepper

½ cup (38 g) chopped lemongrass

4 cloves garlic, minced

1 tbsp (5 g) grated fresh ginger

¼ cup (60 ml) lemon juice

1 tbsp (12 g) brown sugar

⅓ cup (80 ml) cider vinegar

BASTING SAUCE

¼ cup (60 ml) vegetable oil

1 tbsp (11 g) annatto seeds

Salt and freshly ground black pepper

Achara (page 170), for serving

Vinegar Garlic Sauce (page 165), for serving

Using a sharp knife, make 2 shallow cuts on the surface of each piece of chicken. Season with salt and pepper. Set aside.

In a large resealable bag, combine the lemongrass, garlic, ginger, lemon juice, sugar and vinegar. Add the chicken, seal and toss to coat completely. Marinate in the refrigerator for 1 hour.

To make the basting sauce, heat the oil and annatto seeds in a small saucepan over medium heat. Cook, stirring until the oil develops a deep orange color, about 5 minutes. Season with salt and pepper. Remove from the heat and set aside.

Preheat and oil a barbecue grill. Remove the chicken from the marinade and discard the marinade. Place the chicken on the grill. Grill, basting both sides with the sauce, over medium heat for 20 to 25 minutes or until cooked through. Transfer to a plate and let rest for 10 minutes.

Serve with the Achara and Vinegar Garlic Sauce.

PAGKAING—DAGAT
SEAFOOD DISHES

Being a tropical country made up of thousands of islands, it is not surprising that seafood is abundant in Filipino cooking. In fact, seafood is a staple of Filipino cuisine. You can find fishmongers selling fresh seafood, such as fish, crab, squid and shrimp, at any local market. Fish is so abundant that it is commonly salted and dried to preserve it for later. Although dried fish is typically eaten for breakfast with *sinangag* (garlic rice) and dipped in vinegar, it can also be enjoyed for lunch or dinner. *Bangus* (milk fish) is the most popular fish in the Philippines. Although it has a lot of bones, it can be enjoyed fried, smoked, stuffed or even in soups. Tilapia is another popular fish and is normally enjoyed fried or grilled.

FISH ESCABECHE
(SWEET AND SOUR FISH)

Escabeche is a cooking method that involves marinating and cooking meat in an acidic sauce, such as vinegar. This fish escabeche is a Filipino take on the Spanish-originated cooking method. It consists of fried white fish topped with a sweet and sour sauce.

YIELD: 4 SERVINGS

1 whole white fish such as snapper, tilapia, pompano or grouper, approximately 2 lb (900 g), cleaned and scaled

¼ tsp salt

1 tsp all-purpose flour

1 cup (240 ml) canola oil

SWEET AND SOUR SAUCE

¼ cup (60 ml) white vinegar

¼ cup (50 g) sugar

1 tbsp (15 ml) soy sauce

2 tbsp (30 ml) ketchup

½ cup (120 ml) water

2 tbsp (30 ml) olive oil

2 cloves garlic, chopped

1 small onion, sliced

1 (1-inch [2.5-cm]) piece fresh ginger, peeled and julienned

1 small green bell pepper, cut into strips

½ cup (55 g) julienned carrots

1 tbsp (7 g) cornstarch dissolved in 1 tbsp (15 ml) water

Chopped green onions, for garnish

Wash the fish under cold running water and pat dry with paper towels. Make 2 to 3 evenly-spaced shallow cuts between the fin and the tail on both sides of the fish. Season with the salt and lightly coat with the flour.

Heat the canola oil in a wok or large frying pan over medium-high heat. Gently slide the fish into the oil and cook for 4 to 5 minutes on each side, or until crisp and cooked through. Drain the fish well on paper towels.

To make the sauce, combine the vinegar, sugar, soy sauce, ketchup and water in a small bowl. Set aside.

In a skillet, heat the olive oil over medium-high heat. Add the garlic, onion and ginger, and sauté for 2 minutes or until the onion begins to soften. Add the bell pepper and carrots, and sauté for 2 minutes.

Add the sauce to the pan and without stirring, bring the mixture to a boil. Give the cornstarch mixture a final stir and then add to the pan. Stir and cook until the mixture has thickened, about 1 minute.

Place the fish on a serving plate and pour the sauce over the fish. Sprinkle with the chopped green onions.

CRAB IN OYSTER SAUCE

I first learned about this simple dish from my cousin and have been making it for my family ever since. The garlic, ginger and oyster sauce give this dish a flavorful sauce that you can dip the crab in. To take this dish to the next level, you can add vermicelli (bean thread) noodles.

YIELD: 4 SERVINGS

2 tbsp (30 ml) olive oil

2 cloves garlic, chopped

1 (1-inch [2.5-cm]) piece fresh ginger, peeled and cut into matchsticks

2 tbsp (30 ml) oyster sauce

1 tbsp (15 ml) soy sauce

½ cup (120 ml) water

2 medium crab, shells separated and bodies cut into halves

Chopped green onions, for garnish

In a large skillet, heat the oil over medium heat. Add the garlic and ginger, and sauté until the garlic is light brown, about a minute.

Add the oyster sauce, soy sauce and water, and bring to a boil. Add the crab, starting with the body and then top with the shells, if using. Simmer covered until the crab is cooked, about 10 minutes.

Garnish with green onions and serve.

GINATAANG HIPON
(SHRIMP IN COCONUT MILK)

Coconut milk is a popular ingredient in Filipino cooking. Whether it is in a dessert or a main dish, coconut milk is always well used, and this recipe is the perfect example of just that. This simple dish has the perfect amount of creaminess from the coconut milk to complement the spiciness from the chili pepper.

YIELD: 3 SERVINGS

1 lb (450 g) head-on large shrimp

Salt

1 tbsp (15 ml) olive oil

2 cloves garlic, minced

1 (1-inch [2.5-cm]) piece fresh ginger, peeled and julienned

1 Thai chile pepper, chopped

⅔ cup (160 ml) coconut milk

Steamed rice, for serving

Trim the tendrils off of the shrimp with scissors and then rinse under cold running water. Drain, season with salt and then set aside.

Heat the oil in a large skillet over medium heat. Add the garlic and ginger, and sauté until the garlic is lightly browned, about 1 minute.

Add the chile and coconut milk, and bring to a boil.

Add the shrimp and cook for 3 minutes or until the shrimp turn pink. Season with salt to taste. Serve hot with steamed rice.

PAKSIW NA ISDA
(FISH IN VINEGAR SAUCE)

Paksiw na isda is one of the many types of *paksiw* (cooked in vinegar) dishes in Filipino cuisine. In this dish, the fish is cooked in a tangy sauce of vinegar and ginger. Vegetables like eggplant and bitter melon can also be added. Other types of fish like milkfish and snapper may be used in place of short mackerel.

YIELD: 4 SERVINGS

4 (4-oz [113-g]) hasa-hasa (short mackerel), cleaned and scaled

Salt

1 ampalaya (bitter melon), halved, seeded and sliced into thin diagonal pieces (½ inch [13 mm] thick)

1 Japanese eggplant, sliced into thin diagonal pieces (½ inch [13 mm] thick)

1 (1-inch [2.5-cm]) piece fresh ginger, peeled and crushed

2 whole serrano peppers

1 cup (240 ml) white vinegar

1 cup (240 ml) water

Fish sauce, to taste

Steamed rice, for serving

Make 2 to 3 evenly spaced shallow cuts between the fin and the tail on both sides of the fish and then season with salt.

Arrange the fish at the bottom of a heavy pan. Top with the *ampalaya*, eggplant, ginger and peppers. Add the vinegar and water, and without stirring, bring the mixture to a boil. Cook, covered, over medium heat for 10 minutes or until the vegetables are tender and the fish is cooked. Season to taste with fish sauce.

Serve hot with steamed rice.

SARCIADONG ISDA
(FRIED FISH WITH TOMATO SAUCE)

Fish is plentiful in the Philippines, so it is no wonder that there are so many Filipino fish dishes. *Sarciadong isda* is one of these and uses milkfish, one of the most abundant fish in the Philippines. This dish is made by frying the fish and then simmering it in a thick sauce of tomato and egg. Sarciadong isda is also great with tilapia or mackerel in place of milkfish.

YIELD: 4 SERVINGS

1 whole fish (milkfish or Spanish mackerel), approximately 1½ lb (680 g), cleaned, scaled and sliced into 4 pieces

½ tsp salt, plus more to taste

1 tbsp (7 g) all-purpose flour

1 cup (240 ml) vegetable oil

2 tbsp (30 ml) olive oil

2 cloves garlic, chopped

1 small onion, sliced

2 medium tomatoes, chopped

1 tbsp (15 ml) fish sauce

1 cup (240 ml) water

Freshly ground black pepper, to taste

2 eggs, beaten

Chopped green onions, for garnish

Thoroughly wash the fish under cold running water and pat dry with paper towels. Sprinkle the fish with salt and then lightly coat with the flour.

In a wok or frying pan, heat the vegetable oil over medium-high heat. Add the fish and fry until golden brown, about 2 minutes on each side. Drain on paper towels.

In a skillet, heat the olive oil over medium-high heat. Add the garlic, onion and tomatoes, and sauté for 3 minutes. Season with the fish sauce.

Add the water and bring to a boil. Add the fish, reduce the heat to medium and simmer covered for 3 minutes. Season to taste with salt and pepper.

Stir in the eggs and continue to cook for another 2 minutes or until the eggs are set. Transfer to a serving plate. Garnish with the chopped green onions.

SQUID SISIG

Sisig is a dish that is typically made using grilled parts of a pig's head and liver. It is a classic Filipino dish that has many variations depending on the city or region. This recipe is a modern twist on a classic dish that uses squid in place of pork. No matter how the sisig is cooked, it is usually served on a sizzling plate.

YIELD: 2 SERVINGS

2 lb (900 g) squid

Salt

4 tbsp (60 ml) olive oil, divided

2 cloves garlic, chopped

2 tbsp (20 g) chopped shallots

2 red Thai chile peppers, chopped

1 tbsp (15 ml) soy sauce

Freshly ground black pepper

Chopped green onions, for garnish

Lemon wedges, for serving

Clean the squid by pulling the tentacles away from the body. Hold the body and pull out the transparent backbone and discard. Rinse the inside body of the squid in cold water. Slice the body into ½-inch (13-mm) rings. Set aside.

Cut the tentacles away from the guts by slicing just below the eyes; discard the guts and eyes. Push the tentacles outwards and squish the hard beak out. Set the tentacles aside and discard the hard beak.

Pat the squid rings and tentacles dry with paper towels and season lightly with salt.

In a skillet, heat 2 tablespoons (30 ml) of oil over medium-high heat. Add the squid rings and cook until it releases its liquid, about 4 minutes. Using a slotted spoon, remove the squid from the skillet. Discard the liquid.

Using a clean skillet, heat the remaining 2 tablespoons (30 ml) of oil over medium-high heat. Add the squid rings, garlic, shallots, chile peppers and tentacles. Cook until the squid is nicely browned, about 2 minutes. Season with the soy sauce and pepper.

Transfer to a serving or sizzling plate, if using. Sprinkle with chopped green onions and a squeeze of lemon juice.

BISTEK NA BANGUS
(FISH STEAK)

Bistek na bangus is the fish version of the popular Filipino dish *bistek*. Traditional bistek is made with thinly sliced beef that is marinated in soy sauce and *calamansi* or lemon juice, then cooked with fried onions. It uses *bangus* belly instead of beef, but the preparation is otherwise the same. This dish is one that tastes even better the next day, when the fish has had time to absorb the sauce.

YIELD: 6 SERVINGS

3 large boneless bangus belly, cut in halves

MARINADE

¼ cup (60 ml) lemon juice or calamansi juice

¼ cup (60 ml) soy sauce

¼ tsp freshly ground black pepper

½ cup (120 ml) canola oil

3 tbsp (25 g) all-purpose flour

2 medium onions, peeled and cut into rings

½ cup (120 ml) water

1 tsp sugar

Steamed rice, for serving

Place the bangus belly skin side down in a shallow dish.

To make the marinade, combine the lemon juice, soy sauce and pepper in a bowl. Pour over the fish and let marinate for 1 hour. Drain the fish, reserving the marinade.

Heat the oil in a frying pan over medium-high heat. Coat the fish lightly with the flour and fry, in batches, until golden brown, about 3 to 5 minutes per batch. Drain on paper towels and then transfer to a serving plate.

Pour off all but 2 tablespoons (30 ml) of oil from the pan. Add the onion rings and fry for 30 seconds. Add the reserved marinade, water and sugar, and simmer on medium heat for 3 minutes. Pour over the fish.

Serve with steamed rice.

GUISADONG TOGE AT HIPON
(SAUTÉED BEAN SPROUTS AND SHRIMP)

This recipe was created as a result of my attempts at replicating a dish that I tried at a restaurant in the Philippines back in the '80s. The perfectly cooked and crispy sautéed bean sprouts paired with the shrimp and Chinese chives made an impact on me. This dish hits all the high points of that restaurant dish.

YIELD: 2 SERVINGS

½ lb (230 g) shrimp, shelled and deveined

Salt, to taste

1 tbsp (15 ml) olive oil

2 cloves garlic, chopped

1 tbsp (15 ml) soy sauce

4 cups (400 g) bean sprouts, rinsed and drained well

2 oz (56 g) Chinese chives (kuchais), cut into 2-inch (5-cm) lengths

Pepper, to taste

1 tsp sesame oil

Season the shrimp with salt.

Heat the oil in a large skillet over medium-high heat. Add the garlic, and cook until it is lightly browned, about 1 minute.

Add the shrimp and cook, stirring frequently, until the shrimp changes color, about 2 minutes.

Add the soy sauce, bean sprouts and chives. Stir and cook for 1 to 2 minutes. Season with salt and pepper, and drizzle with sesame oil.

DAING NA BANGUS
(FRIED MARINATED MILKFISH)

Daing na bangus is a dish I ate a lot when I was growing up. There was always milkfish marinating in the refrigerator and ready to fry anytime during the day. For breakfast, we would have it with a sunny-side up egg and garlic rice. For lunch or dinner, we would have it with chopped tomatoes and salted eggs. Nowadays, milkfish can be bought frozen, already cleaned and just about ready to cook.

YIELD: 2 SERVINGS

1 large milkfish, fresh or frozen, about 1 lb (450 g), cleaned and butterflied

Salt and freshly ground black pepper

½ cup (120 ml) white vinegar

4 cloves garlic, crushed

3 tbsp (25 g) all-purpose flour

1 cup (240 ml) vegetable oil, for frying

Garlic Rice (page 81), for serving

Achara (page 170), for serving

Vinegar Garlic Sauce (page 165), for serving

Rinse the fish under cold running water. Pat dry with paper towels and sprinkle with salt and pepper.

In a shallow dish, combine the vinegar and garlic. Place the fish in the dish with the meat side down. Cover and marinate in the refrigerator overnight.

Drain the fish and discard the marinade. Dry the fish thoroughly with paper towels and sprinkle all over with the flour.

Heat the oil in a heavy-base frying pan over medium-high heat. Add the fish and fry until brown and crisp, about 4 to 6 minutes, depending on the size of the fish.

Serve with Garlic Rice, Achara and Vinegar Garlic Sauce for dipping.

KANIN AT PANCIT
RICE AND NOODLE DISHES

Whether it is breakfast, lunch or dinner, rice is a staple of every Filipino meal. White rice is mostly served with *ulam* (main dish) for lunch and dinner whereas a typical Filipino breakfast can consist of *sinangag* (garlic rice) with fried egg and either with *longganisa* (sausage), *tocino* (cured meat) or *tuyo* (dried fish). Filipino cuisine also has some one-pot rice dishes, such as paella or *arroz ala valenciana*, that combines rice, meat and vegetables.

Filipinos also love to eat noodles, which were introduced to the Philippines by the Chinese. *Pancit* (noodles) is commonly served at birthday celebrations, as they are a sign of a long and healthy life. There are so many different kinds of pancit with varying types of meats, vegetables, sauces and noodles. The popularity of pancit in the Philippines is obvious from the many restaurants around the country that specialize in this classic Filipino food, as well as the number of variations that depend on the region.

SINANGAG
(GARLIC RICE)

Garlic rice is a popular fried rice dish that is usually served for breakfast along with a fried egg and either cured meat (*tapa, longganisa* or *tocino*), fried fish or even dried fish (*tuyo*). Although typically served for breakfast, this dish can also be enjoyed for lunch or dinner.

YIELD: 4 SERVINGS

3 tbsp (45 ml) vegetable oil

6 cloves garlic, chopped

4 cups (632 g) cooked cold rice

Salt, to taste

Fried egg, for serving

In a wok or heavy-base pan, heat the oil over medium-high heat. Add the garlic and sauté until lightly browned, about 2 minutes.

Add the rice and stir, breaking up any clumps. Cook, stirring frequently, until the rice is hot, about 5 minutes. Season with the salt.

Serve with a fried egg and dried fish or fried cured meat.

CHAMPORADO
(CHOCOLATE RICE PORRIDGE)

Champorado is a sweet chocolate rice porridge that is typically served for breakfast. It is not uncommon to have this delicious porridge alongside *pan de sal* (bread) and *tuyo* (dried fish). It should be topped with a drizzle of evaporated milk, or any other type of milk.

YIELD: 6 SERVINGS

1 cup (185 g) glutinous rice, rinsed and drained

5 cups (1.2 L) water

5 pieces tablea (cacao tablets) or 4 tbsp (28 g) dark cocoa powder dissolved in 1 cup (240 ml) hot water

½ cup (90 g) brown sugar, plus more to taste

½ cup (120 ml) evaporated, soy or almond milk, or half & half cream, plus more for serving

In a pot, bring the rice and water to a boil. Stir, reduce the heat to medium and cook, stirring occasionally, for 20 minutes.

Add the *tablea* and sugar. Continue to simmer, stirring constantly until thick and the chocolate tablets have dissolved completely, about 5 to 8 minutes. Stir in the milk or cream.

Serve hot or cold. Drizzle with more milk or cream.

SEAFOOD PAELLA

Paella is a one-pot Spanish-influenced rice dish that is normally cooked in a shallow, two-handled skillet called a paella pan. There are many versions of paella, but this one is made with seafood. Filipino cuisine is so reliant on seafood and this dish makes good use of it. The best part of this dish is that it is so versatile and you can experiment with which ingredients to include.

YIELD: 6 SERVINGS

3 tbsp (45 ml) olive oil

4 cloves garlic, chopped

1 onion, chopped

2 cups (370 g) long grain rice, rinsed and drained

1 cup (240 ml) tomato sauce

3 cups (700 ml) chicken broth

A pinch of saffron threads

1 red bell pepper, seeded and cut into strips

Salt and freshly ground black pepper, to taste

½ lb (230 g) fresh manila clams, scrubbed

½ lb (230 g) shrimp

½ lb (230 g) squid, cleaned and cut into rings

½ cup (80 g) frozen green peas

2 tbsp (8 g) chopped parsley, for garnish

In a paella pan or a large deep pan, heat the oil over medium-high heat. Add the garlic and onion, and sauté until the onion begins to soften, about 2 minutes. Add the rice and cook, stirring for 1 minute. Stir in the tomato sauce, broth, saffron and bell pepper. Season with salt and pepper. Bring to a boil and cook over medium heat for 10 minutes.

Arrange the clams, shrimp, squid and green peas over the rice. Cook until the shrimp turns pink and the rice is almost done, about 10 minutes.

Remove the pan from the heat and let it sit covered for 10 minutes.

Transfer the rice onto a serving dish. Garnish with the chopped parsley.

SOTANGHON GUISADO
(SAUTÉED BEAN THREAD NOODLES)

Sotanghon guisado is one of the many noodle dishes in Filipino cuisine. This dish uses *sotanghon* (bean thread) noodles and a mixture of fresh vegetables. I like this dish because it's versatile and you can make it your own by adding any meat or vegetable. Sotanghon guisado is great with a squeeze of *calamansi* or lemon juice right before serving.

YIELD: 6 SERVINGS

2 pieces boneless, skinless chicken thighs, cut into thin strips

2 tbsp plus 1 tsp (35 ml) soy sauce, divided

8 oz (230 g) sotanghon noodles (bean thread)

2 tbsp (30 ml) olive oil

2 cloves garlic, chopped

1 small onion, sliced

2 tbsp (30 ml) oyster sauce

½ cup (55 g) julienned carrots

1 cup (150 g) sliced green beans

4 oz (113 g) snow peas, trimmed

1 cup (70 g) sliced green cabbage

1 cup (240 ml) chicken broth

Salt and freshly ground black pepper, to taste

Chopped cilantro, for garnish

In a bowl, combine the chicken and 1 teaspoon (5 ml) of soy sauce. Mix well and then set aside.

Soak the noodles in warm water for 10 minutes, drain and set aside.

Heat the oil in a large skillet over medium-high heat. Add the garlic and onion, and sauté until the onion begins to soften, about 2 minutes. Add the chicken and sauté until it is browned and no longer pink, about 2 minutes. Stir in the 2 tablespoons (30 ml) of soy sauce and oyster sauce.

Add the carrots, green beans, snow peas, cabbage and broth. Cook, covered, until the vegetables are on the crisp side of tender, about 4 minutes.

Add the noodles and cook, stirring, until they have absorbed the sauce. Season with salt and pepper, to taste.

Serve and garnish with the chopped cilantro.

PANCIT PALABOK
(NOODLES IN SPECIAL SAUCE)

Pancit palabok is a very popular noodle dish that is normally eaten as a snack and is a common sight at any special celebration or gathering. This dish consists of noodles with a thick, orange sauce and a wide variety of toppings such as shrimp, tofu, fish flakes, pork rinds and hard-boiled eggs.

YIELD: 10 SERVINGS

1 (16-oz [454-g]) package of special palabok noodles (cornstarch sticks)

4 tbsp (60 ml) olive oil, divided

1 lb (450 g) shrimp, shelled and deveined

2 tbsp (20 g) chopped shallots

2 tbsp (16 g) annatto powder

5 cups (1.2 L) chicken broth

2 tbsp (30 ml) fish sauce, plus more for serving

¼ cup (30 g) cornstarch dissolved in ¼ cup (60 ml) water

8 cups (1.9 L) water

TOPPINGS

1 cup (32 g) crushed chicharon (pork rind cracklings)

11 oz (310 g) firm tofu, fried and cubed

3 hard-boiled eggs, peeled and sliced

¼ cup (25 g) chopped green onions

Lemon wedges

Soak the noodles in cold water for at least 2 hours. Drain and set aside.

In a pan, heat 2 tablespoons (30 ml) of the oil over medium-high heat. Add the shrimp and sauté for 2 minutes or until cooked. Remove the shrimp from the pan and set aside.

Using the same pan, heat the remaining 2 tablespoons (30 ml) of oil. Add the shallots and sauté until soft, about 2 minutes.

Stir in the annatto powder. Add the broth and bring to a boil. Season with the fish sauce. Give the cornstarch mixture a stir and then add it to the broth in the pan, stirring until the sauce thickens, about 2 to 4 minutes. Remove from the heat and set aside.

In a pot, bring the water to a boil. Add the noodles and cook until tender, about 10 minutes. Drain well and transfer to a serving dish.

Spoon the sauce over the noodles and sprinkle with the crushed chicharon. Top with the tofu, shrimp and egg slices. Garnish with the chopped green onions. Serve with the lemon wedges and a small bowl of fish sauce on the side.

LUTUING GULAY
VEGETABLE DISHES

The Filipino diet consists of a lot of meat and seafood and so it is not surprising that there are few vegetarian options. You will often find that vegetables are not the star, but are instead used to balance the dish. Fresh produce can often be found at *palengke*, a public market where vendors sell a wide array of produce, meats and other goods.

Bitter melon is a common vegetable used in Filipino cuisine. As its name implies, it is a unique vegetable due to its very bitter taste. Some other vegetables found in Filipino dishes include Japanese eggplant, okra, *sitaw* (long beans), *patola* (sponge gourd), *kangkong* (water spinach) and chayote.

FRESH LUMPIA
(SPRING ROLLS)

This version of *lumpia* is Chinese-influenced and uses only fresh and healthy ingredients. Fresh lumpia is typically served with all the ingredients separated and then assembled right before eating. It is especially fun to eat and serve at a party because the guests can make their own lumpia and choose their own garnishes (such as cilantro, garlic or crushed peanuts) and seasonings (such as hot sauce, like Sriracha).

YIELD: 20 FRESH LUMPIA

2 tbsp (30 ml) olive oil

2 cloves garlic, minced

1 small onion, chopped

8 oz (230 g) green beans, trimmed and sliced into thin diagonal pieces

2 cups (220 g) shredded carrots

1 (550-ml [540-g]) can bamboo shoot strips, rinsed and drained

2 cups (260 g) shredded singkamas (jicama)

2 cups (140 g) shredded cabbage

1 lb (450 g) firm tofu, cut into ½-inch (13-mm) cubes

½ cup (120 ml) water

Salt and freshly ground black pepper, to taste

LUMPIA SAUCE

¼ cup (45 g) brown sugar

2 tbsp (30 ml) soy sauce

1 cup (240 ml) water

2 tbsp (15 g) cornstarch dissolved in 2 tbsp (30 ml) water

4 cloves garlic, minced

FOR ASSEMBLY

20 (8-inch [20-cm]) frozen spring roll wrappers, thawed and separated

20 Romaine lettuce leaves, washed and dried

¼ cup (34 g) minced garlic

1 bunch cilantro leaves, trimmed

2 tbsp (15 g) crushed peanuts mixed with 2 tbsp (25 g) sugar

Sriracha sauce, optional

Heat the oil in a skillet over medium-high heat. Add the garlic and onion, and sauté until the onion begins to soften, about 2 minutes.

Add the beans, carrots, bamboo shoots, jicama, cabbage and tofu, and sauté for 1 minute. Add the water and cook, covered, over medium heat until the vegetables are on the crisp side of tender, about 10 minutes. Season to taste with salt and pepper. Strain the mixture well through a metal colander.

To make the sauce, combine the brown sugar, soy sauce and water in a saucepan. Bring to a boil. Add the cornstarch mixture and stir continually until thick, about 1 minute. Stir in the garlic. Remove from the heat and set aside.

To assemble, lay a wrapper on a flat surface with one corner facing you. Place a lettuce leaf in the center of the wrapper and then place 2 tablespoons (28 g) of the filling on the leaf. Top with ½ teaspoon of minced garlic, one or two cilantro leaves, ½ teaspoon of peanut mixture and Sriracha, if desired. Fold the bottom part of the wrapper over the filling, tuck in both sides and roll it up tight. Repeat the process for the rest of the filling. To keep them soft and fresh, wrap each lumpia with wax paper.

To serve, remove the wax paper and serve the lumpia with more sauce and crushed peanut mixture.

NOTE: It is important to drain the cooked vegetables to prevent the lumpia from becoming soggy.

GINISANG AMPALAYA
(SAUTÉED BITTER MELON)

Although vegetarian dishes are rare in Filipino cuisine, this *ginisang ampalaya* is vegetarian friendly. Eating bitter melon is an acquired taste as the bitterness can be off-putting to first-time eaters. My husband and I grew up eating this healthy vegetable and have grown to love the taste of bitter melon. If you're not a fan of the taste, there are some ways to get rid of some of the bitterness. One way is to soak the vegetable in salted water. Another trick is to not stir the bitter melon while cooking. But no matter how you cook this dish, it can be enjoyed as a side to a fried meat or fish dish.

YIELD: 4 SERVINGS

1 lb (450 g) ampalaya (bitter melon)

1 tbsp (20 g) kosher salt

2 tbsp (30 ml) olive oil

2 cloves garlic, chopped

1 small onion, chopped

1 small tomato, chopped

1 tbsp (15 ml) fish sauce

2 eggs, beaten

Salt and freshly ground black pepper, to taste

Prepare the bitter melon by cutting each piece in half lengthwise. Using a spoon, scoop out the seeds and scrape off the inner white pith. Slice each half crosswise at a slight angle as thinly as possible.

Place the sliced bitter melon in a large bowl. Cover with water, add the salt and let sit for half an hour. Rinse the ampalaya under cold running water, drain well and set aside.

Heat the oil in a skillet over medium-high heat. Add the garlic and onion, and sauté for 1 minute. Add the tomato and sauté until soft, about 2 minutes. Add the fish sauce and stir to combine.

Add the ampalaya and cook covered, without stirring, until tender, about 3 minutes. Pour the eggs over the ampalaya and cook, without stirring until the eggs have set. Give the mixture a stir and then season with salt and pepper to taste.

Serve as a side dish for fried meat or fish.

PINAKBET
(BOILED VEGETABLES IN ANCHOVY SAUCE)

Pinakbet is a delicious Filipino stew made with pieces of pork and fresh vegetables. There are many versions of pinakbet, each originating from different places in the Philippines. This particular recipe originates from the Ilocos region and uses *bagoong isda* (anchovy sauce) to flavor the sauce. Another popular version is the Tagalog version in which *bagoong alamang* (shrimp paste) is used and the vegetables are sautéed instead of boiled.

YIELD: 6 SERVINGS

8 oz (230 g) banana squash, peeled, seeded and sliced into 1-inch (2.5-cm) cubes

8 oz (230 g) green beans, trimmed

8 oz (230 g) fresh okra

1 ampalaya (bitter melon), halved, seeded and sliced into ½-inch (13-mm) pieces

1 Japanese eggplant, sliced into ½-inch (13-mm) pieces

2 whole serrano peppers

1 large tomato, cut into wedges

1 (1-inch [2.5-cm]) piece fresh ginger, peeled and julienned

1 large onion, peeled and quartered

6 tbsp (90 ml) bagoong isda

1 lb (450 g) sliced Baked Lechon Kawali (Crispy Pork Belly) (page 25), optional

2 cups (475 ml) water

Salt, to taste

Steamed rice, for serving

Arrange the squash at the bottom of a heavy-bottom pan, followed by the green beans, okra, *ampalaya*, eggplant, serrano peppers, tomato, ginger and onion. Top with the bagoong and crispy pork belly, if desired.

Add the water and bring to a boil. Reduce the heat to medium and cook, covered for 5 minutes. Remove the lid, stir the mixture and continue to cook, covered, until the vegetables are tender, about 2 minutes. Season with salt as needed.

Serve hot with steamed rice.

GINATAANG GULAY
(VEGETABLES IN COCONUT MILK)

Ginataang gulay is one of the many Filipino *ginataang* dishes, which translates to "cooked in coconut milk." This creamy dish of banana squash and green beans is made even more flavorful with the addition of shrimp paste. The dish can easily be made vegetarian by omitting the pork.

YIELD: 4 SERVINGS

8 oz (230 g) pork shoulder

4 cups (950 ml) water

1 tsp salt, plus more to taste

2 tbsp (30 ml) vegetable oil

2 cloves garlic, minced

1 small onion, chopped

1 tbsp (15 g) bagoong alamang (shrimp paste)

1 lb (450 g) banana squash, peeled, seeded and cut into 1-inch (2.5-cm) cubes

1 cup (240 ml) coconut milk

8 oz (230 g) green beans, trimmed

Steamed rice, for serving

In a pan, bring the pork, water and salt to a boil. Reduce the heat to medium and cook until tender, about 45 minutes. Remove the pork from the broth, reserving 1 cup (240 ml) of the broth. Let the pork cool slightly and then cut it into ½-inch (13-mm) pieces. Set aside.

Heat the oil in a skillet over medium-high heat. Add the garlic and onion, and sauté until the onion begins to soften, about 2 minutes.

Add the pork and sauté until browned, about 3 minutes. Add the shrimp paste and stir to combine.

Add the squash and reserved broth, and bring to a boil. Lower the heat to medium and cook, covered, for 5 minutes.

Add the coconut milk and green beans, and cook covered, stirring occasionally, until the vegetables are tender, about 10 minutes. Season with salt, to taste.

Serve hot with steamed rice.

GINISANG PATOLA AT MISUA
(SAUTÉED SPONGE GOURD WITH NOODLES)

Patola, also called sponge gourd or *sing gua*, is a green gourd with ridges running down the length of it and is a popular vegetable in Filipino and Chinese cuisine. Once peeled, this vegetable reveals a pale green flesh. Patola can be cooked by stir-frying it or putting it in a soup. One simple way to enjoy this vegetable is in this hearty recipe, which combines it with ground pork and *misua* noodles.

YIELD: 4 SERVINGS

2 tbsp (30 ml) olive oil

2 cloves garlic, chopped

1 small onion, chopped

8 oz (230 g) lean ground pork

1 tbsp (15 ml) fish sauce

2 lb (900 g) patola or sing gua (sponge gourd), peeled and sliced diagonally into 1-inch (2.5-cm) pieces

2 cups (475 ml) chicken broth

2 oz (56 g) misua noodles or Japanese somen noodles

Salt and freshly ground black pepper, to taste

Chopped green onions, for garnish

Heat the oil in a skillet over medium-high heat. Add the garlic and onion, and sauté until the onion begins to soften, about 2 minutes. Add the pork, and sauté until browned, about 3 minutes. Season with the fish sauce.

Add the patola and sauté for 1 minute. Add the chicken broth and bring to a boil. Reduce the heat to medium and cook, covered, for 3 minutes. Stir in the misua and cook until the patola is on the crisp side of tender and the noodles are soft, about 1 minute. Season to taste with salt and pepper.

Garnish with the green onions and serve.

GINISANG KABUTE SA BAYABAS
(SAUTÉED MUSHROOMS WITH GUAVA)

This dish is one of my favorites from my childhood. I have many fond memories of eating this dish and learning how to cook it from my mom. It is a dish that she learned in her hometown of Gapan, Nueva Ecija. This simple and healthy vegetarian dish consisting of stir-fried mushrooms and guava will always be special to me.

YIELD: 3 TO 4 SERVINGS

6 ripe guavas

1½ cups (350 ml) water, divided

2 tbsp (30 ml) olive oil

2 cloves garlic, chopped

1 small onion, chopped

1 tbsp (15 ml) fish sauce, plus more to taste

8 oz (230 g) oyster mushrooms, cleaned and sliced

8 oz (230 g) fresh shiitake mushrooms, cleaned and sliced

Wash the guavas and then cut them in half. Scoop out the seeds and set aside the guava meat.

Transfer the guava seeds to a saucepan. Add 1 cup (240 ml) of water and boil, stirring occasionally over medium-high heat for 10 minutes. Strain the broth and set aside. Discard the seeds.

In a skillet, heat the oil over medium-high heat. Add the garlic and onion, and sauté until the onion begins to soften, about 2 minutes. Add the fish sauce and stir to combine.

Add the mushrooms and remaining ½ cup (120 ml) of water, and cook, covered, stirring occasionally, until tender, about 8 minutes. Add the guava and guava broth, and continue to cook for 2 minutes. Season with fish sauce as needed.

LUMPIANG GULAY
(VEGETABLE SPRING ROLL)

There are many variations of *lumpia* (spring rolls) in Filipino cuisine. Many have different kinds of meat, but this particular version is special in that it uses only vegetables. No matter how lumpia is prepared, it is enjoyed by many and is a staple at any Filipino gathering.

YIELD: 18 SPRING ROLLS

1 cup plus 2 tbsp (270 ml) vegetable oil, divided

2 cloves garlic, minced

1 small onion, chopped

1 cup (110 g) julienned sweet potato

1 cup (110 g) julienned carrots

8 oz (230 g) green beans, trimmed and cut into thin diagonal pieces

2 cups (140 g) shredded green cabbage

8 oz (230 g) firm tofu, cut into ½-inch (13-mm) cubes

1 tbsp (15 ml) soy sauce

1 tbsp (15 ml) oyster sauce

½ cup (120 ml) water

Salt and freshly ground black pepper

18 (8-inch [20-cm]) frozen spring roll wrappers, thawed and separated

Vinegar Garlic Sauce (page 165), for serving

Heat 2 tablespoons (30 ml) of oil in a skillet over medium-high heat. Add the garlic and onion, and sauté until the onion begins to soften, about 2 minutes.

Add the sweet potato, carrots, green beans and cabbage, and sauté for 1 minute. Stir in the tofu, soy sauce, oyster sauce and water, and cook, covered, over medium heat, until the vegetables are on the crisp side of tender, about 2 minutes. Season to taste with salt and pepper. Strain the mixture through a metal colander and let it cool completely.

Lay a wrapper on a plate with one corner facing you. Place 2 tablespoons (28 g) of the filling along the corner closest to you. Roll the wrapper over the filling, tuck in both sides and roll it up tight. Moisten the end with water and press to seal. Repeat the process for the rest of the filling.

In a frying pan, heat 1 cup (240 ml) of vegetable oil over medium-high heat. Fry the lumpia in batches until golden brown, about 2 to 3 minutes for each batch. Drain on paper towels.

Serve with Vinegar Garlic Sauce.

NOTE: This dish can easily be made vegetarian by omitting the oyster sauce.

SABAW
SOUPS

A typical Filipino soup consists of a flavorful clear broth made from boiling meat in a large pot. Pork, beef, shrimp, noodles and vegetables are common ingredients in Filipino soups. While Filipinos like to enjoy a steaming hot bowl of soup all year round, they are especially comforting during the rainy season.

Typically served family-style from one large bowl in the middle of a table, a Filipino soup is known for its heartiness. Souring agents such as tamarind, *santol* (cottonfruit), green mango, guava, *kamias* (*bilimbi*) or *calamansi* are some of the ingredients that can be found in a typical Filipino-style soup. *Sinigang* (sour soup) is a classic example of a Filipino soup with many variations, but is known for its savory and sour taste.

ALMONDIGAS
(MEATBALLS AND NOODLE SOUP)

Almondigas is a hearty soup consisting of meatballs and *misua*. Misua are thin, salted Chinese noodles made from wheat flour that cook quickly. If misua is not available, it can be substituted with Japanese *somen* noodles, since they are quite similar. Like many hearty soups, almondigas is truly a comfort food.

YIELD: 4 SERVINGS

1 lb (450 g) lean ground pork

2 green onions, finely chopped, plus more for garnish

1 egg, beaten

3 tbsp (25 g) all-purpose flour

Salt and freshly ground black pepper

1 tbsp (15 ml) olive oil

2 cloves garlic, minced

1 onion, chopped

8 cups (1.9 L) chicken broth

1 tbsp (15 ml) fish sauce

2 oz (57 g) misua noodles or Japanese somen noodles

In a large bowl, combine the pork, green onions, egg and flour. Season with salt and pepper. Mix together well, then form into 1-inch (2.5-cm) meatballs. Set aside.

Heat the oil in a pot over medium-high heat. Add the garlic and onion. Sauté until the onion begins to soften, about 2 minutes.

Add the broth and fish sauce, and bring to a boil. Drop the meatballs into the boiling broth and simmer for 10 to 15 minutes, or until the meatballs are cooked. Add the misua noodles and cook until soft, about 3 minutes. Season with fish sauce (or salt) and pepper, to taste.

Garnish with the chopped green onions. Serve hot.

SINAMPALUKANG MANOK
(CHICKEN TAMARIND SOUP)

Sinigang is one of the signature dishes of the Philippines, so it's no wonder there are so many different ways to cook it. This is another way to make sinigang that makes use of the juices of green or unripe tamarind pods, giving the soup a sour taste. The green tamarind pods are boiled for a few minutes and then strained. They are then added to the soup at the last stage of the cooking process. Although fresh green tamarind pods are seldom available outside of the Philippines, frozen ones can be used instead and are much more common.

YIELD: 6 SERVINGS

3 lb (1.3 kg) mixture of bone-in chicken thighs and drumsticks

Salt

8 oz (227 g) frozen unripe tamarind pods or 1 (40-g) packet of tamarind seasoning mix

8 cups (1.9 L) water, divided

2 tbsp (30 ml) olive oil

1 (1-inch [2.5-cm]) piece fresh ginger, peeled and julienned

1 medium onion, sliced

1 tbsp (15 ml) fish sauce, plus more for serving

8 oz (230 g) green beans, trimmed

2 whole serrano peppers

8 oz (230 g) tamarind leaves or baby spinach

Steamed rice, for serving

Season the chicken with salt.

If using tamarind pods, combine the tamarind and 2 cups (475 ml) of water in a saucepan. Cook over medium-high heat for 10 minutes or until the tamarind is soft. Using the back of a spoon, mash the softened tamarind. Strain the juice into a bowl and set aside, discarding the seeds and shells.

Heat the oil in a stockpot over medium-high heat. Add the ginger and onion, and sauté until the onion begins to soften, about 2 minutes. Add the chicken and cook, stirring for 4 minutes, or until chicken is no longer pink. Add the fish sauce and stir.

Add 6 cups (1.4 L) of water, if using tamarind pods, or 8 cups (1.9 L) of water, if using seasoning mix, and bring to a boil. Reduce the heat to medium and cook covered until the chicken is tender, about 25 minutes. Add the green beans and serrano peppers, and cook until the beans are tender, about 5 minutes.

Stir in the tamarind juice or seasoning mix and simmer for 5 minutes. Add the tamarind leaves or spinach. Season to taste with fish sauce or salt.

Serve with steamed rice and fish sauce on the side.

NOTE: A convenient alternative to using tamarind pods is to use the readily available packets of tamarind seasoning mix that you can find in the Asian section of the supermarket.

BULALO
(BONE MARROW SOUP)

Bulalo is a soup made of beef shank, marrow bones and vegetables. During a visit to the Philippines, I had the opportunity to have a bowl of this hearty soup in Tagaytay, which is famous for this soup. This soup is especially enjoyable when you are able to cook the beef for a long time and it becomes fall-off-the-bone tender. The marrow is also able to incorporate into the soup better this way, which gives a more flavorful broth.

YIELD: 4 SERVINGS

2 lb (900 g) bone-in beef shank, cut into bite-size pieces

12 cups (2.9 L) water

2 medium onions, peeled and halved

1 tsp kosher salt, plus more to taste

1 tsp whole peppercorns

1 large potato, peeled and cubed

2 cobs corn, cut into 2-inch (5-cm) pieces

4 bok choy, cut into halves and rinsed

4 whole ripe saba bananas (burro bananas), peeled and cut in half crosswise

Steamed rice, for serving

Fish sauce, for serving

In a large stockpot, bring the beef shank and water to a boil. Add the onions, salt and peppercorns. Reduce the heat and simmer covered for 1 hour, or until the meat is fork tender.

Add the potato and corn, and cook for 10 minutes. Add the bok choy and *saba*, and cook for 5 minutes. Season to taste with salt.

Serve hot on its own or with steamed rice and fish sauce on the side.

PANCIT MOLO
(PORK DUMPLING SOUP)

Pancit molo is a traditional Filipino soup consisting of shredded chicken and pork dumplings in a delicious broth. It is similar to Chinese wonton soup since both contain pork dumplings that are dropped into the soup during cooking. *Pancit* is the Tagalog word for noodles, but ironically, this soup does not contain any type of noodle.

YIELD: 6 SERVINGS

BROTH

1 lb (450 g) skinless, bone-in chicken breast

2 lb (900 g) chicken bones

12 cups (2.9 L) water

1 tsp salt

1 onion, peeled and halved

½ tsp whole peppercorns

FILLING

1 lb (450 g) lean ground pork

½ lb (230 g) shrimp, shelled, deveined and finely chopped

2 tbsp (12 g) finely chopped green onions

1 tbsp (15 ml) soy sauce

¼ tsp salt

¼ tsp freshly ground black pepper

1 egg, lightly beaten

FOR THE SOUP

50 wonton wrappers

2 tbsp (30 ml) olive oil

2 cloves garlic, minced

1 onion, chopped

1 tbsp (15 ml) soy sauce

Salt and freshly ground black pepper, to taste

4 cups (364 g) broccoli florets

Chopped green onions, for garnish

To make the broth, combine the chicken breast, chicken bones, water, salt, onion and whole peppercorns in a stockpot. Bring the mixture to a boil and simmer for 30 minutes, or until the chicken is cooked. Remove the chicken breast from the broth, let it cool and then shred the meat. Strain the broth and set aside.

To make the filling, combine the ground pork, shrimp, green onions, soy sauce, salt, pepper and egg in a bowl. Mix until well combined.

Fill the center of the wonton wrapper with 1 tablespoon (14 g) of filling. Wrap the edges around the filling. Repeat with the rest of the wrappers and filling. Set aside.

Heat the oil in a pot over medium-high heat. Add the garlic and onion, and sauté until the onion begins to soften, about 2 minutes. Add the chicken and soy sauce. Stir and then add the reserved broth. Season with salt and pepper. Bring to a boil and then drop the wontons into the broth. Cook for 5 minutes or until the wontons float to the top. Add the broccoli and cook for 3 minutes.

Ladle the soup into serving bowls and top with chopped green onions.

FISH TINOLA
(FISH IN LEMONGRASS SOUP)

Tinola is a type of soup in the Philippines that consists of some type of meat and vegetables in a ginger-flavored broth. It is hearty enough to eat as a main entrée, but can also be served as an appetizer. This fish tinola is a version from the Visayan region of the Philippines and has a clear broth flavored with onions, tomato and lemongrass.

YIELD: 4 SERVINGS

1½ lb (680 g) fish steak (red snapper, cod or bass)

Salt and freshly ground black pepper

8 cups (1.9 L) water

1 small onion, chopped

1 medium tomato, chopped

1 (2-inch [5-cm]) piece fresh ginger, peeled and julienned

2 stalks lemongrass, cut into segments and crushed

2 tbsp (30 ml) fish sauce

2 whole serrano peppers

1 cup (30 g) baby spinach

Season the fish with salt and pepper.

In a pot, combine the water, onion, tomato, ginger, lemongrass and fish sauce. Bring the mixture to a boil. Reduce heat to medium and cook for 15 minutes. Add the fish and serrano peppers, and simmer until the fish is cooked, about 10 minutes.

Stir in the spinach and simmer for 1 minute. Season with salt and pepper.

LOMI SOUP

Lomi soup is a Chinese-influenced soup consisting of thick noodles, chicken or pork, shrimp, fish balls and vegetables in a thick broth. There are many ways to make this dish, but this version is the closest to how I remember it growing up in the Philippines. It is such a flexible dish and each household has their own way of making it. Nothing beats a hot and filling bowl of lomi soup on a cold, rainy day!

YIELD: 6 TO 8 SERVINGS

1 lb (450 g) fresh Shanghai noodles

½ lb (230 g) pork tenderloin, sliced into thin strips

2 tbsp (30 ml) soy sauce, divided

½ lb (230 g) shrimp, shelled and deveined

Salt, to taste

2 tbsp (30 ml) olive oil

2 cloves garlic, chopped

1 small onion, chopped

½ cup (55 g) julienned carrots

1 cup (70 g) shredded napa cabbage

8 cups (1.9 L) chicken broth

½ lb (230 g) fish balls, cut in half

Freshly ground black pepper, to taste

¼ cup (30 g) cornstarch dissolved in ½ cup (120 ml) water

2 eggs, beaten

Chopped green onions, for garnish

Rinse the noodles under cold running water. Drain and set aside.

In a bowl, combine the pork and 1 tablespoon (15 ml) of soy sauce. Cover and marinate in the refrigerator for at least 1 hour. Season the shrimp with salt and then set aside.

Heat the oil in a pot over medium-high heat. Add the garlic and onion, and sauté until the onion begins to soften, about 2 minutes.

Add the pork and marinade, and sauté until browned and no longer pink, about 2 minutes. Add the carrots, cabbage and 1 tablespoon (15 ml) of soy sauce, and stir. Add the chicken broth and bring to a boil.

Add the fish balls, shrimp and noodles, and cook for 5 minutes. Season to taste with salt and pepper.

Give the cornstarch mixture a stir, and slowly add it to the broth in the pan, stirring until the soup thickens, about 1 to 2 minutes. Immediately pour in the eggs in a steady stream to form flower patterns on the surface.

Serve hot, and garnish with the green onions.

SINIGANG NA ISDA SA MISO
(FISH IN TAMARIND MISO SOUP)

Sinigang is a soup dish characterized by its sourness. The most common souring ingredient used is green or unripe tamarind but other fruits like green mango, *calamansi*, *santol* (cottonfruit) and *kamias* (*bilimbi*) are also used. This particular sinigang combines the sour taste of tamarind and the salty and rich flavor of miso. The addition of mustard leaves completes this tasty and flavorful soup.

YIELD: 6 TO 8 SERVINGS

2 salmon heads, about 2 lb (900 g) each, cut in half, or 4 salmon steaks

Salt, to taste

5 unripe tamarind pods or 1 (1.76-oz [50-g]) packet tamarind seasoning mix

8 cups (1.9 L) water, divided

1 (1-inch [2.5-cm]) piece fresh ginger, peeled and julienned

1 large onion, sliced

1½ lb (680 g) daikon, peeled and sliced diagonally into ½-inch (13-mm) pieces

2 tbsp (30 ml) fish sauce, plus more for serving

3 tbsp (51 g) miso paste

2 cups (112 g) chopped mustard leaves (gai choy), or baby spinach

2 large tomatoes, cut into wedges

2 whole serrano peppers

Steamed rice, for serving

Season the fish with salt. Set aside.

If using tamarind pods, in a saucepan, combine the tamarind and 2 cups (475 ml) of water. Boil over medium heat for 10 minutes or until the tamarind is soft. Using the back of a spoon, mash the softened tamarind. Strain the juice into a bowl and set aside, discarding the seeds and shells.

Bring 6 cups (1.4 L) of water, if using tamarind pods, or 8 cups (1.9 L) of water, if using seasoning mix, to a simmer in a stockpot. Add the ginger, onion, daikon and fish sauce, and cook until the daikon is tender, about 5 minutes.

Add the fish and cook for 4 minutes. Add the tamarind juice or seasoning mix, and cook for 1 minute. Stir in the miso paste, mustard leaves, tomatoes and serrano peppers, and return to a boil. Season to taste with salt.

Serve hot with steamed rice and fish sauce.

PORK IN GUAVA SOUP

This soup was one of my favorites when growing up in the Philippines. I learned to make this simple soup from my mom at a young age. Here in Canada, guava is seasonal, so guava soup base mix can be used when fresh guava isn't available. However, nothing beats the taste of real fresh guava in this soup!

YIELD: 6 TO 8 SERVINGS

10 ripe guavas

12 cups (2.9 L) water, divided

3 lb (1.3 kg) pork side ribs, cut into segments

1 tsp salt

Fish sauce, to taste, plus more for serving

4 cups (120 g) baby spinach

2 whole serrano peppers

Steamed rice, for serving

Wash the guava and then cut the pieces in half. Scoop out the seeds and set the guava meat aside.

Transfer the guava seeds to a saucepan. Add 1 cup (240 ml) of water and bring to a boil, stirring occasionally over medium-high heat for 10 minutes. Strain the guava broth and set aside. Discard the seeds.

In a large pot, bring 11 cups (2.6 L) of water and the pork to a boil. Add the salt and simmer covered for 1 hour, or until the meat is fork tender.

Add the guava meat and guava broth, and continue to simmer for 5 minutes. Season with the fish sauce. Add the spinach and serrano peppers, and continue to cook for 1 minute.

Serve with steamed rice and fish sauce on the side.

MUNGGO SOUP
(MUNG BEAN SOUP)

I grew up eating a stewed version of this dish but I was recently introduced to the soup version during one of my visits to the Philippines. My friend raved about this dish, so I had to try it out. The same ingredients are used as the stew version, except *munggo* soup isn't as thick and is topped with *chicharon* (pork rind cracklings). Smoked fish flakes can be used in place of pork to add some extra smoky flavor to the dish. Or, if you'd prefer, the soup can easily be made vegetarian by leaving out the pork.

YIELD: 6 SERVINGS

8 oz (230 g) pork shoulder

12 cups (2.9 L) water, divided

1 tsp salt, plus more to taste

1 cup (207 g) mung beans, rinsed

2 tbsp (30 ml) olive oil

2 cloves garlic, chopped

1 small onion, chopped

2 tbsp (30 g) sautéed shrimp paste

2 cups (60 g) trimmed pepper leaves or baby spinach

2 whole serrano peppers

1½ oz (42 g) chicharon (pork rind cracklings), for topping

In a pan, bring the pork, 4 cups (950 ml) of water and salt to a boil. Reduce the heat and cook over medium heat until tender, about 45 minutes. Remove the pork from the broth, reserving the broth. Let the pork cool slightly and then cut into ½-inch (13-mm) pieces. Set aside.

In a stockpot, bring the mung beans and 8 cups (1.9 L) of water to a boil. Reduce the heat and cook over medium-high heat until tender, about 30 minutes. Set aside.

In a Dutch oven or a heavy pan, heat the oil over medium-high heat. Add the garlic and onion, and sauté until the onion begins to soften, about 2 minutes.

Add the pork and sauté until browned, about 3 minutes. Add the shrimp paste and stir to combine. Add the boiled mung beans plus the reserved pork broth, and cook for 5 minutes. Stir in the pepper leaves and serrano peppers, and season to taste with salt.

Ladle soup into serving bowls, and top with chicharon.

SUWAM NA HALAAN
(CLAM IN GINGER SOUP)

Suwam na halaan is a simple dish consisting of clams cooked in a broth of ginger and onions. This comforting and nourishing soup uses leafy greens such as *malunggay*, pepper leaves or spinach. It is one of my family's easy-to-make favorites and using fresh clams is what makes this dish so simple but so delicious.

YIELD: 4 SERVINGS

2 tbsp (30 ml) olive oil

1 (1-inch [2.5-cm]) piece fresh ginger, peeled and julienned

1 onion, sliced

1 tbsp (15 ml) fish sauce

2 lb (900 g) fresh manila clams, scrubbed

4 cups (950 ml) water

Salt, to taste

2 cups (112 g) trimmed malunggay, pepper leaves or spinach

Heat the oil in a pot over medium-high heat. Add the ginger and onion, and sauté until the onion begins to soften, about 2 minutes.

Add the fish sauce, clams and water. Cook, covered, until the shells open, about 7 minutes.

Season with salt. Stir in the malunggay or pepper leaves.

MERIENDA
SNACKS

Snacking is such an everyday part of Filipino culture that there is even a special name for it. *Merienda* is a light meal that Filipinos enjoy late in the morning or in the afternoon. It typically includes some kind of hot drink, like coffee or hot chocolate. Having a good merienda helps to refuel in between meals.

A variety of different foods ranging from sweet to savory can be served for merienda. In the Philippines, snacks like fish balls, *ukoy* (shrimp and vegetable fritters) and *banana cue* (caramelized fried banana) may be bought all day from street vendors and roadside stalls. There are even food carts and *taho* (silken tofu with sago pearls) vendors that regularly come around the neighborhood.

LUMPIANG SHANGHAI
(PORK SPRING ROLLS)

Lumpiang Shanghai is a finger food that you can find at most Filipino feasts or celebrations. These Chinese-influenced spring rolls are typically filled with ground meat and vegetables. I love making them for parties because they are always a big hit—these crunchy rolls are especially delicious when dipped in hot sauce or sweet and sour sauce.

YIELD: 24 PIECES

FILLING

1 lb (450 g) lean ground pork

⅓ cup (37 g) grated carrots

3 tbsp (30 g) minced shallots

1 tsp garlic powder

1 tbsp (15 ml) soy sauce

1 tsp sugar

1 tsp freshly ground black pepper

1 egg, slightly beaten

LUMPIA

24 (6-inch [15-cm]) frozen spring roll wrappers, thawed and separated

Vegetable oil, for deep-frying

Sweet and Sour Sauce (page 166), for serving

To make the filling, combine the ground pork, carrots, shallots, garlic powder, soy sauce, sugar, pepper and egg in a bowl. Mix thoroughly.

Lay a wrapper on a plate with one corner facing you. Place 1 tablespoon (14 g) of the filling along the corner closest to you. Roll the wrapper over the filling, tuck in both sides and roll it up tight.

Moisten the end with water and press to seal. Repeat the process for the rest of the filling.

Deep-fry a few pieces at a time in hot oil until golden brown and cooked through, about 4 to 6 minutes. Drain on paper towels to remove excess oil.

Serve hot with Sweet and Sour Sauce.

BANANA CUE
(CARAMELIZED FRIED BANANA)

Banana cue is a sweet snack that you can find being sold in the streets of the Philippines. Although the use of skewers is optional, they make it easier to serve and eat. These fried caramelized bananas were one of my favorite afternoon snacks when I was growing up. I would walk to the corner store and would have a choice of *camote cue* (caramelized sweet potato), or banana cue. The two were both cooked the same way and were both delicious!

YIELD: 3 SERVINGS

1 cup (240 ml) vegetable oil

6 ripe saba bananas (burro bananas), peeled

¼ cup (45 g) brown sugar

3 (12-inch [30-cm]) bamboo skewers, optional

Heat the oil in a large heavy pan over medium heat. Gently add the bananas and fry until lightly browned, about 2 minutes on each side.

Sprinkle half of the sugar on top of the bananas. Turn the bananas over and sprinkle the other side with the rest of the sugar. Continue frying, until the sugar has caramelized, about 3 minutes. Turn and move the bananas around until completely coated with the caramelized sugar.

Cool lightly and thread each skewer, if desired, with 1 to 2 caramelized fried bananas.

NOTE: Thai bananas may also be used if burro bananas are not available.

GINATAANG MAIS
(STICKY RICE *AND* CORN *IN* COCONUT MILK)

Ginataang mais is a simple snack consisting of glutinous rice that is cooked in coconut milk with kernels of corn and sugar. This dish was one of my favorite *merienda* (afternoon snacks) growing up, and I would usually enjoy this hearty snack when I came home from school. In addition to being served as a snack, ginataang mais can also be served as a dessert.

YIELD: 6 SERVINGS

4 cups (950 ml) coconut milk

½ cup (96 g) glutinous rice, rinsed and drained

1½ cups (248 g) whole kernel corn

½ cup (100 g) sugar

¼ cup (60 ml) half & half cream, optional

In a saucepan, combine the coconut milk and rice, and bring to a boil over medium-high heat.

Cook, stirring regularly, over low heat until the rice is cooked, about 25 minutes.

Add the corn and sugar, and continue cooking for 5 minutes.

Serve hot or cold and drizzled with cream, if desired.

PALITAW
(BOILED RICE CAKE)

Palitaw is a sticky and chewy snack that is coated in coconut, sugar and sesame seeds. It is usually eaten as a *merienda*, but is sweet enough to satisfy those dessert cravings as well. These glutinous rice patties are easy to make as they are simply formed and then boiled. Palitaw means "to rise" or "to float," and that is exactly how you know when they are ready!

YIELD: 24 PIECES

¼ cup (50 g) sugar

2 tbsp (18 g) roasted sesame seeds

2 cups (320 g) glutinous rice flour

13 cups (3.2 L) water, divided

1 cup (60 g) grated coconut or sweetened coconut flakes

In a small bowl, combine the sugar and sesame seeds. Set aside.

In a large bowl, combine the rice flour and 1 cup (240 ml) of water, and mix to form a dough. Add additional flour a little bit at a time if it's too sticky, or add water if it's too dry. Knead the dough until smooth and stretchy, and then form into 1-inch (2.5-cm) balls. Flatten each ball into a patty, about 2 inches (5 cm) in diameter.

In a pot, bring 12 cups (2.9 L) of water to a boil. Drop the patties in batches into the boiling water and cook until they float to the top, about 2 minutes for each batch. Using a slotted spoon, scoop the rice patties and transfer them to a plate. Cool the patties for 2 minutes.

Coat the patties completely with the coconut flakes and then serve sprinkled with the sugar-sesame mixture.

MARUYA
(BANANA FRITTERS)

Maruya is a popular street food consisting of *saba* bananas (burro bananas) that are coated in batter, deep-fried and served with a sprinkle of sugar. They are crispy on the outside and tender and sweet on the inside. A variation uses sweet potato instead of saba.

YIELD: 8 SERVINGS

1 cup (120 g) all-purpose flour

1 tsp baking powder

½ tsp salt

1 cup (240 ml) milk

1 egg, lightly beaten

2 cups (475 ml) canola oil

4 ripe saba bananas (burro bananas), peeled and sliced in half lengthwise

2 tbsp (25 g) sugar

In a bowl, whisk together the flour, baking powder and salt. Add the milk and egg, and whisk until smooth.

Heat the oil in a large frying pan over medium-high heat. Dip each banana in the batter and fry until golden brown, about 2 minutes for each side. Drain on paper towels. Roll the fritters in sugar while they are still warm and serve immediately.

KALABASANG UKOY
(SQUASH FRITTERS)

There are many different ways to cook *ukoy*, but my favorite is *kalabasang ukoy*, which uses squash as its main ingredient. The use of squash gives you ukoy that is crunchy on the outside but soft and tender on the inside. These fritters can be served as an appetizer or snack, and are especially delicious when dipped in Vinegar Garlic Sauce.

YIELD: 8 FRITTERS

½ cup (60 g) cornstarch

½ cup (60 g) all-purpose flour

1½ tsp (6 g) baking powder

1 tsp salt

¾ cup (180 ml) water

2 cups (410 g) grated butternut squash

8 oz (230 g) tiny shrimp

2 tbsp (12 g) chopped green onions

2 cups (475 ml) canola oil, for frying

Vinegar Garlic Sauce (page 165), for serving

To make the fritters, combine the cornstarch, flour, baking powder, salt and water in a large mixing bowl. Mix until smooth. Add the squash, tiny shrimp and green onions. Mix well.

Heat the oil in a wok or frying pan over medium-high heat. Place 2 tablespoons (28 g) of the mixture in a saucer and then gently slide the mixture into the hot oil. Fry until golden brown and crispy, about 3 minutes. Drain on paper towels.

Serve with the Vinegar Garlic Sauce.

NOTE: Small fish can be used in place of shrimp.

BAKED CHICKEN EMPANADA

Empanadas are fried or baked stuffed pastries that are popular among Filipinos. They are on many café menus throughout the Philippines and can be enjoyed with a cup of hot coffee. Empanadas are very versatile since you can fill them with different meats or vegetables to fit your taste. Ground beef, pork, chicken and potato are common empanada fillings.

YIELD: 15 EMPANADAS

FILLING

2 tbsp (30 ml) olive oil

2 cloves garlic, chopped

1 small onion, chopped

2 boneless, skinless chicken thighs, cut into small cubes

1 tsp soy sauce

¼ cup (32 g) diced carrots

½ cup (110 g) diced potatoes

½ cup (80 g) frozen green peas

½ cup (120 ml) water

¼ cup (37 g) raisins

1 tbsp (15 ml) oyster sauce

Salt and freshly ground black pepper, to taste

3 hard-boiled eggs, peeled and sliced

DOUGH

1½ cups (180 g) all-purpose flour

2 tbsp (25 g) sugar

¼ tsp baking powder

¼ tsp salt

½ cup (120 g) cold unsalted butter, cut into cubes

2 tbsp (30 ml) cold water

1 egg, beaten

To make the filling, heat the oil in a skillet over medium heat. Add the garlic and onion, and sauté for 2 minutes, or until the onion begins to soften. Add the chicken and cook until brown, about 2 minutes. Stir in the soy sauce.

Add the carrots, potatoes, peas and water, and cook, covered, for 3 minutes.

Add the raisins and oyster sauce, and cook, stirring occasionally, for 1 minute or until the vegetables are cooked. Season with salt and pepper. Remove from the heat, drain and cool completely.

Preheat the oven to 400°F (204°C). Line a baking sheet with parchment paper.

To make the dough, combine the flour, sugar, baking powder and salt in a medium bowl. Add the butter and using a fork, break up the butter into the flour mixture until it is fully incorporated. Add the water and egg, and mix until a soft dough is formed.

Take heaping tablespoons (14 g) of dough and form into balls. On a floured surface and using a rolling pin, flatten the dough balls into thin circles, about ⅛-inch (3-mm) thick.

Place about a tablespoon (14 g) of the filling in the center of the dough. Top with a slice of hard-boiled egg. Wet the edge of one side of dough with water and then fold over to form a half moon shape. Seal the edge by gently pressing them together. Using a fork, gently press the edges to form ridges. Continue with the rest of the dough and filling.

Place the empanadas on the prepared pan. Generously brush the tops and sides with egg wash (whisk 1 egg with 1 tablespoon [15 ml] of cold water) and bake for about 20 to 25 minutes or until lightly browned.

PANGHIMAGAS
DESSERTS

There are so many kinds of desserts in the Philippines. These desserts may be found in a typical Filipino bakery that sells a wide range of pastries, sweets and desserts. *Leche flan* (caramel custard) is a custard made of eggs and condensed milk with a soft caramel topping and is considered one of the most popular desserts in the Philippines. This decadent dessert is usually served on special occasions.

Coconut is a common ingredient in Filipino desserts and it is typical to find shredded coconut or coconut milk as an ingredient. Desserts are not restricted to after mealtime; these desserts are enjoyed throughout the day and it is not unusual to have dessert as a snack.

LECHE FLAN
(CARAMEL CUSTARD)

Leche flan is one of those desserts that you will find served at any gathering, holiday or special occasion. Leche flan is normally made in a *llanera*, which is a special mold for leche flan, but practically any pan or mold can be used. This recipe uses individual ramekins because they are more easily served. There are different ways to make this delicious dessert, but no matter how or what ingredients are used, this dessert is loved by anyone who tries it!

YIELD: 6 SERVINGS

¾ cup (150 g) sugar

2 whole eggs

8 egg yolks

1 (10-oz [300-ml]) can sweetened condensed milk

1 (12-oz [354-ml]) can evaporated milk

¼ tsp finely grated lime

½ tsp vanilla extract

Position the oven rack in the middle of the oven. Preheat the oven to 325°F (163°C).

In a heavy saucepan, melt the sugar over medium-high heat. Cook, without stirring, until the sugar starts to caramelize, about 5 minutes.

Immediately divide the hot caramel into 6 (7-oz [200-ml]) ramekins, tilting the ramekins side to side to fully coat the bottom of the ramekins with the caramel. Set aside.

In a large bowl, lightly beat the eggs and egg yolks. Add the sweetened condensed milk, evaporated milk, grated lime and vanilla. Beat the mixture until well blended.

Pour the mixture through a medium-mesh sieve into a liquid measuring cup. Divide the mixture evenly among the ramekins.

Place a kitchen towel in the bottom of a large roasting pan, then place the prepared ramekins on top of the kitchen towel. Pour enough hot water in the roasting pan to come halfway up the sides of the ramekins.

Carefully place the roasting pan in the oven. Bake the custards in the hot water bath for 25 to 30 minutes, or until the custard is set. Cool the custard in the water bath for 20 minutes and then refrigerate to chill for several hours or overnight.

To serve, run a knife around the side of the ramekin and quickly turn the custard into a serving plate. Pour any remaining caramel sauce in the ramekin over the custard.

BIKO
(SWEET RICE CAKE)

Biko is a quintessential Filipino dessert made of glutinous rice, coconut milk and brown sugar. It can be eaten as a *merienda* (snack) or dessert. It can also be served during special events such as birthday parties or town fiestas. These sweet treats can be enjoyed as is, or with a topping of *latik* (coconut curds), a brown residue created when coconut milk is simmered. Although traditional biko is cooked on a stovetop, this recipe simplifies the process by using a rice cooker. It makes the cooking process much easier and the result is just as good.

YIELD: 12 SERVINGS

2 cups (384 g) glutinous rice, rinsed and drained

2 cups (475 ml) water

2 cups (360 g) dark brown sugar

1 (14-oz [400-ml]) can coconut milk

Lightly grease the sides and bottom of an 8-inch (20-cm) square baking pan. Set aside.

Combine the rice and water in a rice cooker. Cover and turn on the rice cooker. Once the rice is cooked, set aside for 10 minutes.

In a heavy pan, dissolve the sugar in the coconut milk over medium-high heat. Continue to boil, stirring until thick, about 5 minutes. Add the cooked rice and cook, stirring over medium heat until very thick and hard to stir, about 10 minutes.

Spread the rice mixture on the prepared pan and let cool to set.

MANGO TURON
(FRIED BANANA MANGO ROLL)

Turon is a classic street food made with a slice of banana rolled in brown sugar, covered with a wrapper, and then fried. This recipe takes this classic dish to the next level by adding a slice of mango. The result is a delicious roll that is crunchy on the outside while sweet and soft on the inside.

YIELD: 8 SERVINGS

1 tbsp (12 g) brown sugar

¼ tsp cinnamon

8 (8-inch [20-cm]) frozen spring roll wrappers, thawed and separated

4 ripe saba bananas (burro bananas), peeled and sliced in half lengthwise

1 ripe mango, sliced into thin strips

1 cup (240 ml) vegetable oil

Vanilla ice cream, for serving (optional)

In a small bowl, combine the sugar and cinnamon, and mix well.

Lay a wrapper on a plate with 1 corner facing you. Roll 1 slice of *saba* in the sugar mixture and then place it along the corner of the wrapper closest to you. Top the banana with 2 strips of mango. Roll the wrapper over the banana, tuck in both sides and roll it up tight. Moisten the end with water and press to seal. Repeat the process for the rest of the bananas and mangoes.

Heat the oil in a frying pan over medium-high heat. Fry the turon in batches until golden brown, about 3 to 4 minutes. Drain on paper towels.

Serve as is or with vanilla ice cream.

GINATAANG BILO BILO
(STICKY RICE BALLS IN COCONUT MILK)

Ginataang bilo bilo is a sweet dessert consisting of glutinous rice balls, sweet potatoes, purple yams, *saba* bananas and jackfruit cooked in coconut milk. This dish is sometimes called *ginataang halo halo*, meaning "mixed and cooked in coconut," which is a fitting name considering the variety of ingredients used. This sweet treat is enjoyed hot, as a dessert or snack for *merienda*.

YIELD: 6 TO 8 SERVINGS

SAGO

8 cups (1.9 L) water

½ cup (50 g) small sago (tapioca pearls)

RICE BALLS

1 cup (150 g) glutinous rice flour

½ cup (120 ml) water

COCONUT MILK

2 (14-oz [400-ml]) cans coconut milk

2 cups (475 ml) water

1 cup (133 g) cubed sweet potatoes (kamote)

1 cup (133 g) cubed purple yams (ube)

2 ripe saba bananas (burro bananas), peeled

1 cup (151 g) sliced fresh jackfruit (langka)

½ cup (100 g) sugar

To make the sago, in a pot, bring the water to a boil. Add the sago and cook, stirring occasionally, on medium heat, until soft and translucent, about 25 minutes. Remove the pot from the heat and let it sit for 5 minutes. Transfer the sago to a strainer and rinse under cold running water. Drain well and set aside.

To make the rice balls, combine the rice flour and water in a bowl, and mix to form a dough. Form a teaspoon of the dough into a smooth ball. Repeat with the remaining dough, yielding 26 balls. Cover and set aside.

In a saucepan, combine the coconut milk and water. Bring the mixture to a boil, stirring occasionally. Add the sweet potatoes and yams, and cook for 5 minutes.

Add the saba, jackfruit and rice balls and cook for 3 minutes. Add the sago and sugar, and cook for 2 minutes. Serve in a bowl, hot or cold.

BUKO SALAD
(YOUNG COCONUT SALAD)

Buko salad is a popular dessert among Filipinos. It is one of those desserts that you are almost guaranteed to find at a Christmas or birthday party. The use of canned and frozen ingredients in this recipe makes this dish easily accessible and easy to put together.

YIELD: 6 TO 8 SERVINGS

1 (6-oz [180-ml]) can cream (Nestlé is recommended) or thick cream (Carnation is recommended), shaken well

½ cup (120 ml) sweetened condensed milk, plus more to taste

3 (16-oz [454-g]) packages of frozen shredded young coconut, thawed and drained

1 (30-oz [836-g]) can Fiesta fruit cocktail, drained

1 (14-oz [398-ml]) can pineapple chunks, drained

1 (12-oz [340-g]) jar nata de coco (sweet coconut gel), drained

1 (12-oz [340-g]) jar kaong (sweet sugar palm), drained

In a large mixing bowl, whisk the cream and the sweetened condensed milk. Add the young coconut, fruit cocktail, pineapple chunks, *nata de coco* and *kaong*. Gently stir the mixture until well combined.

Taste and add more condensed milk as needed. Cover and chill for at least 4 hours before serving.

NOTE: Drain all bottled or canned ingredients really well. If possible, drain overnight in the refrigerator.

FILIPINO MACAROONS

Filipino macaroons differ from other types of macaroons in that they use flour. These sweet and chewy mini coconut muffins contain the perfect amount of flaked coconut—it is not overpowering nor is it too sweet.

YIELD: 36 MINI MUFFINS

⅓ cup (75 g) unsalted butter, at room temperature

⅓ cup (65 g) sugar

3 eggs

1 tsp vanilla extract

1 (10-oz [300-ml]) can sweetened condensed milk

½ cup (60 g) all-purpose flour, sifted

1 cup (60 g) sweetened flaked coconut

Preheat the oven to 350°F (177°C). Line a 36 mini-muffin pan with paper cups.

In a bowl, cream the butter until light and fluffy. Gradually add the sugar. Add the eggs one at a time, beating well after each addition.

Add the vanilla and condensed milk, and mix well. Add the flour and beat until smooth. Stir in the flaked coconut.

Pour into the prepared muffin pan. Bake for 20 to 25 minutes, or until the top is golden brown and a cake tester comes out clean.

MANGO ICE CREAM

This mango ice cream makes use of the Philippines' most popular and abundant fruit: the mango. This soft and creamy ice cream is no-churn and does not require an ice cream machine. With only three ingredients, this recipe is perfect for those looking for an easy way of making some sweet and delicious ice cream at home.

YIELD: 8 SERVINGS

2½ cups (476 g) diced fresh ripe mango

1 (10-oz [300-ml]) can sweetened condensed milk

2 cups (475 ml) whipping cream

Place the mango in a food processor and process until smooth. Transfer the pureed mango into a bowl. Add the condensed milk and whisk until combined. Set aside.

In a large bowl, beat the cream until stiff peaks form. Add the mango mixture to the bowl and gently fold it in.

Spoon the mixture into a container. Cover loosely with a plastic wrap, making sure the plastic covers the entire top surface. This will prevent the formation of ice crystals on the surface. Freeze for at least 8 hours or overnight.

PICHI PICHI
(STEAMED SWEET CASSAVA)

Pichi pichi is a jelly-like dessert or snack made of grated cassava, sugar and water. It is steamed, and then coated with grated coconut. This well-known Filipino delicacy is a simple treat that will satisfy your sweet tooth!

YIELD: 12 SERVINGS

1 (16-oz [450-g]) package frozen grated cassava, thawed

1 cup (200 g) sugar

2 cups (475 ml) water

1½ cups (90 g) grated coconut

Combine the grated cassava, sugar and water. Mix until the sugar has completely dissolved.

Fill 12 silicone baking cups or regular muffin tins with the cassava mixture. Place on a steamer and steam until slightly firm and clear, about 1 hour. Let it cool for 20 minutes and then refrigerate for 1 hour or until set.

Using a big serving spoon, scoop the pichi pichi from the molds and then coat completely with the grated coconut.

SAWSAWAN AT ENSALADA

DIPPING SAUCES AND ACCOMPANIMENTS

A typical Filipino meal usually comes with some type of *sawsawan* (dipping sauces) or accompaniment to enhance flavor and add texture to the main dishes. A sawsawan can be sweet, salty or even sour. Popular examples of sawsawan include vinegar or *calamansi*-based sauces. Pickled vegetables or *ensaladas* (salads) can also be found as accompaniments at a typical Filipino dinner table. Even when eating at a restaurant, it is common to be served sawsawan or accompaniments with the meal, especially for fried or grilled meat, seafood and soups.

Whether it is a simple fish sauce for *sinigang* (sour soup) or a sawsawan of soy sauce and calamansi for fried fish, one thing is certain: Filipino food isn't quite the same without the right sawsawan!

VINEGAR GARLIC SAUCE

This tangy and garlicky sauce is one of the most used dipping sauces in Filipino cuisine. It is a common sight to see a saucer of this dipping sauce served alongside foods such as *lumpiang prito* (vegetable spring roll), *lechon kawali* (deep-fried pork belly) or *kalabasang ukoy* (squash fritters).

YIELD: ⅓ CUP (80 ML)

⅓ cup (80 ml) white vinegar

2 cloves garlic, minced

½ tsp salt

¼ tsp freshly ground black pepper

2 small Thai red chile peppers, chopped

In a small bowl, combine the vinegar, garlic, salt, pepper and chile peppers. Mix thoroughly.

SWEET AND SOUR SAUCE

Sweet and sour sauce is fundamental in both Asian and Filipino cuisine. It can be used as a dipping sauce for fried foods like *lumpiang Shanghai* (pork spring rolls), or be used along with vegetables to garnish *escabeche* (fried fish). No matter where it is used, sweet and sour sauce is a mainstay in Filipino cooking.

YIELD: 1 CUP (240 ML)

In a small saucepan, whisk together the vinegar, sugar, ketchup and soy sauce, and bring to a boil over medium-high heat. Stir in the cornstarch mixture and cook until the sauce thickens, about 1 minute.

¼ cup (60 ml) white vinegar

¼ cup (50 g) sugar

½ cup (120 g) ketchup

1 tbsp (15 ml) soy sauce

1 tsp cornstarch dissolved in 1 tbsp (15 ml) water

ACHARANG PIPINO
(PICKLED CUCUMBER)

Filipino cuisine is known for its use of sour flavors, so it's no surprise that sliced, pickled cucumbers are a well-loved accompaniment. This recipe is easy to make and the crispy, refreshing cucumbers pair exceptionally well with fried or grilled meat or fish.

YIELD: 2 SERVINGS

In a medium bowl, combine the vinegar, sugar, salt and pepper. Mix thoroughly until the sugar has completely dissolved. Add the cucumber and toss to combine flavors. Chill for at least 1 hour before serving.

½ cup (120 ml) white vinegar

¼ cup (50 g) sugar

½ tsp salt

¼ tsp freshly ground black pepper

1 English cucumber, sliced thinly

ACHARA
(PICKLED GREEN PAPAYA)

Achara is a condiment made with pickled, grated green papayas. The combination of the sweet and sour makes it the perfect accompaniment to meat or fish dishes. One bite of this crunchy and refreshing condiment will leave you wanting more!

YIELD: 6 CUPS (900 G)

4 cups (550 g) grated green papaya

1 cup (125 g) grated carrots

1 small red bell pepper, seeded and cut into strips

1 small green bell pepper, seeded and cut into strips

1 (2-inch [5-cm]) piece fresh ginger, peeled and cut into matchsticks

1 small onion, peeled and sliced thinly

¼ cup (75 g) kosher salt

½ cup (75 g) raisins

PICKLING SOLUTION

2½ cups (600 ml) white vinegar

1¾ cups (350 g) sugar

Sterilize 3 (16-oz [500-ml]) mason jars with lids. Set aside.

In a large bowl, combine the papaya, carrot, bell peppers, ginger and onion. Sprinkle with the salt and mix thoroughly. Cover and let stand for at least 2 hours.

Drain the vegetables and using a cheesecloth, squeeze out as much liquid as you can. Add the raisins to the papaya mixture and mix well. Pack loosely in the sterilized mason jars. Set aside.

To make the pickling solution, combine the vinegar and sugar in a saucepan. Boil until the sugar dissolves, about 7 to 10 minutes. Remove from the heat and let cool slightly. Pour over the vegetables in the jars and let cool at room temperature. Cover the jar tightly and refrigerate for 2 to 3 days before consuming.

TOMATO AND SALTED EGG SALAD

This tomato and salted egg salad is a popular side dish. The salted duck eggs combined with the tomatoes create a unique blend of flavor and texture. The strong flavors in this salad make it the perfect accompaniment to fried or grilled dishes.

YIELD: 2 TO 3 SERVINGS

2 salted duck eggs, shelled and diced

2 medium tomatoes, diced

2 tbsp (12 g) chopped green onions

1 tsp fish sauce

Freshly ground black pepper

In a medium bowl, combine the eggs, tomatoes and green onions. Add the fish sauce and pepper. Stir gently until combined.

ENSALADANG MANGGA
(GREEN MANGO SALAD)

Mangoes are so abundant in the Philippines, it is no wonder that this delicious fruit is used in so many Filipino dishes. This *ensaladang mangga* dish makes use of unripe green mangoes known for their sour taste. This accompaniment is the perfect side dish to any fried or grilled food, adding a depth of flavor with its sour and sweet taste.

YIELD: 4 SERVINGS

In a bowl, combine the tomato, mangoes, onion and cilantro. Mix thoroughly. Top with the shrimp paste.

1 large tomato, diced

2 green or semi-ripe fresh mangoes, diced

1 small onion, diced

1 tbsp (3 g) chopped fresh cilantro

2 tbsp (30 g) sautéed shrimp paste

ENSALADANG TALONG
(EGGPLANT SALAD)

This Filipino-style eggplant salad is the perfect side dish to accompany any grilled or fried meat or fish. Fans of eggplant will enjoy this fresh and versatile salad. It can be made several different ways depending on what ingredients are available and personal preference. No matter how this salad is prepared, it's always a hit!

YIELD: 4 SERVINGS

4 large Chinese eggplants

1 tbsp (15 ml) fish sauce

2 tbsp (30 ml) white vinegar

1 large tomato, diced

1 onion, diced

Salt and freshly ground black pepper, to taste

2 tbsp (12 g) chopped green onions

Grill or boil the eggplants until soft, about 3 minutes per side if grilling or 20 to 25 minutes if boiling. Let them cool then gently peel the skin off, leaving the stems intact. Arrange the eggplants on a platter and set aside.

In a bowl, combine the fish sauce, vinegar, tomato and onion. Mix well. Spread the mixture evenly over the eggplants and then season with salt and pepper. Sprinkle the top with green onions.

ACKNOWLEDGMENTS

First, I would like to thank you, the reader. I hope you get as much from reading this book as I did from creating it. I would also like to thank the followers of my blog, for without you all, none of this would be possible.

To my husband, William, for helping me prepare the ingredients and for cleaning up after my messes. Your honest critiques, love, patience and support helped me so much throughout this process.

To my son Kendal, the other half of Salu Salo Recipes, for taking care of the technical side of the blog and for your tremendous help in creating this book. The encouragement you give me every day helps keep me going.

To my youngest son Kenard, for your valuable and thoughtful advice. Thank you for taste testing and for the input that helped me refine these recipes.

To my oldest son Kendrick and daughter-in-law Clara for tasting my creations, giving your honest feedback and offering moral support throughout the process.

I want to also thank the rest of my family and friends who shared their cooking techniques and provided helpful advice.

Thank you to Elizabeth, Will, Laura and everyone at Page Street Publishing for this amazing opportunity, your hard work and for believing in this project.

Last but not least, I want to thank my mom and dad who ignited my passion for food and shaped and influenced my cooking style.

ABOUT THE AUTHOR

Liza Agbanlog works as a special education assistant and a part-time food blogger. Before immigrating to Canada from the Philippines, Liza worked as a high school math teacher for 10 years, where she earned her bachelors of science in education.

Liza and her family immigrated to Canada in 1992. She spent the next seven years being a full-time mom to three young boys. During this period, it was initially difficult for her to find the time and ingredients to cook authentic Filipino food. Eventually, she was able to adapt and simplify the dishes she enjoyed in the Philippines using easily available ingredients.

In 2012, Liza started her food blog Salu Salo Recipes to compile the recipes she had accumulated throughout the years. Through her blog, she hopes to help other families who may share similar experiences throughout the world.

Liza now lives in Vancouver, Canada, with her husband and youngest son.

INDEX

C